Bread and Bidding

Brian Senior

B.T.Batsford Ltd, *London*

First published 1991
First Batsford edition 1997

ISBN 0 7134 8142 0

A CIP catalogue record for this book is
available from the British Library.

Printed by Redwood Books, Trowbridge,
Wiltshire.

Published by B.T.Batsford Ltd
583 Fulham Road, London
SW6 5BY

INTRODUCTION

Anyone who is attending, or has recently completed, a course of beginner's lessons in bridge may feel that it is all very difficult. I would have to confess that competitive auctions, with both sides bidding, can at times be far from easy, as you are not always in a position to make the bid you would like to make and have to use your judgement to decide on the next best call instead. Judgement is something which can only come from experience, but given a free run, there is a set of basic rules to follow which should get you to a sensible contract most of the time while you acquire that experience. Ah, you say, but there are so many rules to remember and they vary so much from one situation to another. That is true, it is always difficult to remember a whole series of unconnected facts. The trick is to understand the underlying logic of the bidding, so that you can ask yourself one simple question before making each bid: what am I trying to achieve? — i.e. what do I want to tell partner? If you have that understanding you will be able to bid intelligently, even if you do forget the precise point count promised by a particular bid.

The aim of this book is to impart a better understanding of basic Acol bidding. While each section will have a brief introduction, this will be done largely through a series of exercises. We all learn better from our mistakes, and if you get many of the answers wrong you should not worry: anyone who tries all the exercises then studies the correct answers, and most importantly the reasoning behind them, cannot fail to improve their bidding.

Concentrate on those areas in which you did badly until you can see where you were going wrong. You will come out all the better for the experience. Good luck.

SECTION ONE
THE UNCONTESTED AUCTION

The Opening Bid

The purpose of the bidding is for the two partners to exchange sufficient information about the strength and shape of their hands such that eventually one of them is able to decide what suit, if any, should be trumps, and how high to go, i.e. whether to settle for a part-score, go for game, or even try for a slam. Obviously, since even a one-level contract requires your side to make at least seven of the thirteen tricks, you must have a reasonable number of high cards in your hand before you want to get involved in the bidding at all. An average hand would contain one ace, one king, one queen, one jack, etc, and a hand roughly one king above average is strong enough to open the bidding with one of a suit. As a general guideline, two such hands facing each other should usually have a good chance of making a game contract.

Of course it is not only the high-card strength but also the shape of a hand which is important — a long suit, for example, can be a source of several extra tricks. What is needed is a method of comparing a king with two queens, or an ace with a king and a jack, a four-card suit with a six-card suit, and so on, so as to decide whether or not a particular hand is worth an opening bid. This is done using the point count. When you pick up a hand you allocate point values as follows:

each ace	—	4 points
each king	—	3 points
each queen	—	2 points
each jack	—	1 point

Also, each card over four in any suit is worth one extra point, so for a five-card suit add one point, a six-card suit two points, two five-card suits two points, and so on.

If the total comes to thirteen or more, one king over average, you can open with one of a suit. Note that, although you are contracting to make seven tricks, you do not have to have seven tricks in your own hand, you assume that partner will contribute something. Also, remember that these points

are solely an aid to evaluating your hand, you don't actually score anything
for holding them.

There are other opening bids, the requirements for which will be listed later.
If your hand does not qualify for any of these but does come to the magic
figure of thirteen or more points then you should open one of a suit.

Having decided to open the bidding with one of a suit, the next question
is, which suit? There are two points to consider. Firstly, the best trump suit
will usually prove to be the one of which you and your partner together
hold the most, preferably at least eight to give you a clear majority. Secondly,
if you have more than one suit and partner doesn't like the first one you
bid, you are going to want to bid the second one next to give him a choice
without sending the bidding to too high a level. These considerations lead
to the following rules.

With one suit longer than any other, that is the suit you open however weak
it may be. For example, holding:

$$♠ \ 10 \ 7 \ 6 \ 3$$
$$♡ \ A \ K \ Q$$
$$♢ \ K \ 10 \ 6$$
$$♣ \ A \ 7 \ 2$$

open one spade, not one heart, even though the spades are weak and the
hearts so strong. High cards will usually take tricks whatever suit is trumps,
extra tricks can be made with small cards if they are trumps, as you can
trump in once you are void of another suit.

With two five-card suits open the higher-ranking one, spades with spades
and hearts, hearts with hearts and clubs, and so on. The one exception is
that with five clubs and five spades you do better to open one club. The
reason is this, if partner does not like the first suit you bid he is usually
going to suggest an alternative of his own. Now, you know that you want
one of your suits to be trumps and want to show him your second suit.
Compare these two sequences:

(a)	opener	responder	(b)	opener	responder
	1♢	2♣		1♡	2♣
	2♡			2♢	

In sequence (a), if responder wants to give preference to opener's first suit
— diamonds — he must go to the three level to do so. In sequence (b), he

3

can choose either suit while staying at the two level, either by passing or by bidding two hearts, so the second sequence is clearly more economical.

Try it with opener having spades and clubs, and you will see the reason for the exception to the general rule.

With two four-card suits you open the lower ranking, e.g. open one heart with:

♠ A J 7 3
♡ K Q 6 4
♢ 10 3
♣ A Q 2

This time you have a pretty flat hand with no strong preference for any particular suit. The only reason you did not open 1NT is that you have too many points to do so (as we shall see later). What could be more natural than to bid 1NT at your next opportunity? This tells partner that you have a balanced hand which was too strong to open 1NT — perfect. If you are only going to show one of your suits, it is better to bid the one which makes it easier for partner to bid the other one if he holds it. Say you have four hearts and four spades as above, if you open one heart partner can easily bid one spade if he wishes to, so you find your spade fit. If on the other hand you open one spade, he may not be strong enough to raise the level of the bidding by calling two hearts, so a heart fit could be missed.

With three four-card suits open the middle of three touching suits, i.e. one hearts with a singleton club, and one diamond with a singleton spade, but one club with non-touching suits, i.e. a red singleton. It is a sad fact that if you are short in a suit that is the suit partner is most likely to be long in. By following the above rule, you are always opening a suit lower ranking than the one you are missing where possible, so making it easy for partner to bid that suit if he wants to, and you will always have a convenient rebid available yourself for the next round.

Special Opening Bids

1NT — This shows 12–14 high card points (HCPs) and a flattish hand. A flat, or balanced, hand is one with neither a very long nor a very short suit, so you have no strong preference as to what should be trumps. The permitted shapes are 4-3-3-3, 4-4-3-2 and 5-3-3-2, but in the last case the five-card suit should be a weak one as otherwise you would have a preference. 1NT is a very precise opening bid and it is essential that you have both the right point count *and* the right shape before you use it. For example:

♠ Q 6 2
♡ K J 4 3
♢ A J 7 4
♣ Q 10

Two clubs — This is an artificial bid, in other words it says nothing at all about your holding in clubs, indeed you may hold no clubs at all. Two clubs simply shows a very strong hand, promising either 23 plus HCPs or a hand which wants to get to game even opposite nothing, e.g.

♠ A K J 4
♡ A Q J
♢ A K J 10 7
♣ J

Two of a suit other than clubs — These openings show a long strong suit, at least five cards, and a strong hand with at least eight fairly sure playing tricks so long as you get to choose the trump suit. Although high cards are obviously important, it is also essential to have the eight tricks, rather than any specific point count, to make one of these opening bids. Also, perhaps you are afraid that if you open with a one bid and everybody passes, you may have missed game, e.g.

♠ A K Q 10 7 3
♡ A K J 4
♢ 7 2
♣ 8

2NT — Shows a balanced hand with 20–22 HCPs. The permitted shapes are as for 1NT except that you could hold quite a good five-card suit and still open 2NT, for example:

♠ A Q 7
♡ A 7
♢ A Q J 10 4
♣ K J 3

Three of a suit — Shows a weak hand, less high-card strength than is required to open at the one level, but a long and reasonably strong suit, usually of at least seven cards. The idea is that the long suit should keep you out of too much trouble, while the high level of the bidding will make life very difficult for your opponents, who more often than not will have the majority of the high cards, e.g.

♠ K Q 10 8 7 6 4
♡ J 3
◇ 7
♣ 10 6 4

3NT — This is a very rare opening showing a completely solid seven- or eight-card minor suit with little or nothing outside. If partner has bits and pieces in the other suits he can leave it in and hope that you can run nine tricks, while if he is weak the opposition have to start at an uncomfortably high level, e.g.

♠ J 6
♡ 7
◇ A K Q J 7 4 2
♣ 10 8 3

Four of a suit or five of a minor — Similar to three of a suit but with extra playing strength, e.g.

♠ A K J 10 8 7 5 4
♡ 6
◇ J 10 4
♣ 5

Even higher opening bids are possible, but are so rare as to be not worth worrying about at this stage.

QUIZ ONE
The Opening Bid

What is the correct opening bid with each of the following hands?

1) ♠ Q J 6 4
    ♡ Q J 6 4
    ◇ A 7 3
    ♣ K 4

2) ♠ J 10 7 3 2
    ♡ A K Q J 7
    ◇ Q 3
    ♣ 2

3) ♠ K J 6 4
    ♡ K J 6 4
    ◇ A Q 3
    ♣ K 4

4) ♠ A J 10 7 3
    ♡ K Q 6
    ◇ 7 2
    ♣ 9 3 2

5) ♠ A J 10 7 3
    ♡ K 4
    ◇ 7
    ♣ A J 10 7 3

6) ♠ A K Q 10
    ♡ J 9 6 3 2
    ◇ K 4 2
    ♣ 7

7) ♠ Q J 6 2
    ♡ 7
    ◇ K Q 5 4
    ♣ A J 3 2

8) ♠ 7
    ♡ A Q J 4
    ◇ A J 6 3
    ♣ K 10 7 4

9) ♠ A Q
    ♡ K 6 3
    ◇ J 10 7 4 2
    ♣ K 3 2

10) ♠ Q 3
    ♡ Q 6 3
    ◇ A Q 10 9 4
    ♣ K 3 2

Bread and Butter Bidding

SOLUTIONS TO QUIZ ONE
The Opening Bid

1) ♠ Q J 6 4
♡ Q J 6 4
◇ A 7 3
♣ K 4

1NT. This is a balanced hand within the required point count (12–14) so 1NT describes it perfectly. Note that if instead you bid one of your suits you may have trouble finding a satisfactory rebid on the next round.

2) ♠ J 10 7 3 2
♡ A K Q J 7
◇ Q 3
♣ 2

One spade. The higher ranking of two five-card suits even though your hearts are stronger. You can bid hearts next to give partner a choice, more convenient than bidding hearts then spades, as he will be able to choose either suit and still stay at the two level.

3) ♠ K J 6 4
♡ K J 6 4
◇ A Q 3
♣ K 4

One heart. Balanced, but too strong for 1NT, so the *lower* of two four-card suits intending to bid no-trumps next time to show your general hand type.

4) ♠ A J 10 7 3
♡ K Q 6
◇ 7 2
♣ 9 3 2

Pass. 10 HCPs plus one for the fifth spade only brings the total up to eleven — not enough to open the bidding.

5) ♠ A J 10 7 3
♡ K 4
◇ 7
♣ A J 10 7 3

One club. Usually with two five-card suits you open the higher, this is the exception. On the next round you are going to want to bid your second suit to give partner a choice. Just imagine that partner is going to respond in one of your short suits. 1♣ – 1◇ – 1♠ is a lot more convenient than 1♠ – 2◇ – 3♣, isn't it?

6) ♠ A K Q 10
♡ J 9 6 3 2
◇ K 4 2
♣ 7

One heart. Length before strength. It is the number of trumps you hold between you that is most important, not how strong they are.

7) ♠ Q J 6 2
♡ 7
◇ K Q 5 4
♣ A J 3 2

One club. With three non-touching four-card suits, open one club. Now partner can bid any other suit at the one level if he doesn't like clubs. If he bids diamonds or spades you are happy, while if he bids hearts, you can bid one spade — still at the one level.

8) ♠ 7
♡ A Q J 4
◇ A J 6 3
♣ K 10 7 4

One diamond. The middle of three touching suits. Again, whatever partner responds you are comfortably placed.

9) ♠ A Q
♡ K 6 3
◇ J 10 7 4 2
♣ K 3 2

1NT. 13 HCPs and 5-3-3-2 shape, which counts as balanced when the five-card suit is weak — as here. With the same shape and strength but a strong five-card suit you would have a distinct preference for that suit as trumps so would bid it.

10) ♠ Q 3
♡ Q 6 3
◇ A Q 10 9 4
♣ K 3 2

One diamond. The other side of the coin. With the good suit you open it despite the flat shape and 13 HCPs.

One of a Suit — The First Response

When partner's opening bid is one of a suit, he can have anything from a bare thirteen points up to about twenty or twenty-one — just short of a two bid. If you have a very weak hand you will have to pass, but if there is even the slightest chance of game being on, you should respond, so as not to risk missing the rich bonus for bidding and making a game. The minimum combined point counts needed for game are roughly as follows:

3NT	—	25–26 points
4♡/4♠	—	26–27 points
5♣/5♢	—	28–29 points

These point counts are total points including distributional points.

From this we can see that you should be responding to partner's opening bid whenever you have about six or more points — far less than is needed to open the bidding — just in case he has a maximum opener.

If you are to play in a trump contract you will need not only sufficient high-card strength but also an adequate number of trumps. While a strong seven-card fit may occasionally suffice, this usually means at least eight cards between the two hands for four hearts/four spades and preferably nine for five clubs/five diamonds. Experience has shown that where an eight-card fit is available the major suit game, four hearts/four spades, will usually be easier to make than 3NT.

For example:

```
        ♠ A Q 7 4       N      ♠ K J 3
        ♡ Q J 6 4           E  ♡ K 9 8 7
        ♢ K 3       W          ♢ Q 4
        ♣ J 7 2         S      ♣ K Q 6 4
```

3NT will quickly be defeated by diamond leads, while four hearts has a good chance of just losing the three missing aces. The difference is that a trump suit provides a way of controlling the diamond suit.

However, unless the hands are very unbalanced or one suit is completely unprotected, 3NT can often prove easier to get than five clubs/five diamonds, even though there is a trump fit. This is because in a minor suit game only two tricks can be lost as against four in 3NT. So the bidding is aimed firstly at finding a major suit fit, secondly at no-trumps, and only as a last resort at a minor suit game. If you have insufficient strength for game, however, this consideration no longer applies as obviously a minor suit part-score is just as easy to make as one in a major suit at the same level. The "pecking order" of responses is then as follows:

1) Support partner's major suit where possible — whenever you hold four of them.
2) Bid a new four-card major at the one level or any new five-card suit at the two level.
3) Raise partner's minor suit.
4) Bid no-trumps, occasionally even with four-card support for a minor suit but a completely flat hand (4-3-3-3) and every suit covered, e.g. bid 1♣ - 1NT with:

♠ Q 7 6
♡ Q 8 3
♢ K 10 5
♣ J 6 4 2

Supporting Partner's Suit

As partner's opening bid only guaranteed a four-card suit, responder usually needs four cards to be able to show immediate support. This ensures that the partnership will always have the magic number of eight trumps between them.

The exception would be a hand like:

♠ A 6 4
♡ 7
♢ Q 6 3 2
♣ 8 5 4 3 2

where to raise a one spade opening to two spades is likely to reach a better contract than would a response of 1NT. Just think about playing 1NT on a heart lead.

Having found a suit with which you are both happy, there is no need to look elsewhere, and the only remaining problem is to decide how high to go. Should you try for game or settle for a safe part-score?

Responder can support opener's suit by raising it to the two level, three level, four level, or indeed even higher. All these bids show a liking for the suit, the difference is in the strength of responder's hand. He makes what is called a **limit bid**, however high he raises opener's suit he is saying "partner, I like your suit and I have sufficient strength to think that this is the limit to which we can go unless you have more than you have promised me". The opener can now look at his hand and decide whether he has sufficient extra strength to bid on or whether he should just pass. In terms of points, responder's bids show roughly the following:

1♡ – 2♡ = 6–9 points, for example:
  ♠ A 4 3
  ♡ Q 7 4 2
  ♢ 6 5
  ♣ J 8 7 4

1♡ – 3♡ = 10–12 points, for example:
  ♠ A 4 3
  ♡ Q 7 4 2
  ♢ A 5
  ♣ J 8 7 4

1♡ – 4♡ = 13–15 points, for example:
  ♠ A Q 3
  ♡ Q 7 4 2
  ♢ A 5
  ♣ J 8 7 4

These point counts are the same whichever suit is involved, but only when both players are bidding the same one.

You will remember that when you are opening the bidding you are allowed to add points for the shape of the hand. So you can here, except that instead of adding points for length you add points for short suits. When you have plenty of trumps a short suit somewhere can be very useful, because you can trump partner's losing cards in that suit. You can only count these points when you have a trump fit because, without one, the shortage may prove to be of no value, or indeed to be a positive liability if it is facing partner's favourite suit. The awards are: five points for a void (no cards), three points for a singleton (one card), and one point for a doubleton (two cards). So, in response to one heart:

♠ 7 4   is worth 5 HCPs + 1 for the doubleton =
♡ K J 6 3   6 Total Points.
♢ J 7 6 5
♣ 10 4 2

♠ 7　　　　　　　　　is worth 5 HCPs + 3 for the singleton =
♡ K J 6 3　　　　　　8 Total Points.
◇ J 7 6 5 3
♣ 10 4 2

♠ None　　　　　　　is worth 5 HCPs + 5 for the void =
♡ K J 6 3 2　　　　　10 Total Points.
◇ J 7 6 5 3
♣ 9 4 2

Bidding No-trumps

As you would expect, a bid of no-trumps shows a balanced hand, one with
no strong preference for one suit over any other. It also denies four cards
in partner's suit, otherwise you would have supported him. A bid of no-
trumps tells partner almost everything about the shape of your hand, but
what about the strength? Just as when you are supporting partner's suit, so
when bidding no-trumps, you can do so at various levels and again the more
you bid the more high cards you promise.

1 suit – 1NT	=	6–9 HCPs
1 suit – 2NT	=	11–12 HCPs
1 suit – 3NT	=	13–15 HCPs

With exactly 10 HCPs you can either downgrade your hand and respond
1NT or can change the suit.

It is very important that when bidding no-trumps or raising partner's suit,
you bid the full limit of your hand immediately. If, for example, partner
opens one heart and you respond 2NT, you are showing specifically 11 or
12 HCPs. If you bid 2NT when you actually have 14 HCPs, then you have
misled your partner and can hardly complain if he misjudges his next bid.

Bidding a New Suit

Things are not quite so straightforward when you have to bid a new suit.
When bidding no-trumps or supporting partner's suit you could afford to
jump the bidding because you knew where you were going and the only
remaining question was, how high? It would be madness to jump from say
one heart to three spades to show 11 HCPs and four spades — i.e. a limit
bid. If partner did not like spades he would have to bid a suit that he did

like, but you might then be over the limit and would often go down in your contract. Limit bids then, are not a practical solution and the actual rule is that even a simple change of suit, such as 1♡ – 1♠, compels the opener to bid again — so there is no need to jump as responder will always be getting a second chance. 1♡ – 1♠ could be bid on:

♠ K J 7 4	or	♠ K Q 10 9 7 6
♡ 7 6		♡ 8
◇ Q 10 4 2		◇ A Q J 6 5
♣ J 7 3		♣ K

or anything in between. Responder hopes to be able to make a more definite decision at his next turn to call after he has heard his partner's rebid.

So, a new-suit response at the one level, e.g. 1♡ – 1♠ or 1♣ – 1♡, shows at least four cards in the bid suit and at least six points. As when opening the bidding, you should bid your longest suit first whenever possible, and with two suits of equal length, the higher ranking of five-card suits, but the cheaper of four-card suits. For example, in response to one diamond, bid one heart with:

> ♠ K 10 7 4
> ♡ A 6 4 2
> ◇ J 7 3
> ♣ 8 6

but one spade with:

> ♠ K 10 7 4 2
> ♡ A 8 6 4 2
> ◇ 7 3
> ♣ 8

A new suit response at the two level pushes the bidding up higher, meaning that at least one extra trick will be required to make your contract. A general rule of bidding is that whenever a player drives the bidding to a higher level, he must hold the extra strength to produce the extra trick(s). Therefore, a new suit response at the two level promises at least 9 HCPs and a five-card suit, or 10 plus HCPs with only a four-card suit. In practice responder will usually have a five-card suit for a two-level bid, as he has not only failed to support his partner's suit but has also bypassed no-trumps, so is unlikely to have a balanced hand, e.g.

♠ Q 10 3
♡ 7 4 2
◇ A Q J 3
♣ Q 10 9

would respond 2NT, rather than two diamonds, to one heart.

One important point here is that a two-level response promises 9 plus HCPs, but that does not mean that you must bid at the two level every time you have 9 plus HCPs. Remember that a new suit at the one-level shows *6 plus HCPs* — no upper limit — and can be made even with a very good hand. What I mean is that when the ranking order of the suits *forces* you to go to the two level, e.g. partner opens one diamond and you want to bid clubs, *then* you need at least 9 HCPs to do so. Over one diamond, bid two clubs with·

♠ 7 3
♡ K Q 4
◇ J 6 3
♣ A 10 6 4 2

but one spade with:

♠ A 10 6 4 2
♡ K Q 4
◇ J 6 3
♣ 7 3

The eagle-eyed reader may have spotted a conflict between two rules:

1)   you always respond with 6 plus HCPs.
2)   a new suit at the two level promises 9 plus HCPs.

What are you to do with six, seven or eight points if bidding your longest suit would mean going to the two level? The answer is that you must find an alternative at the one level. Over one heart you could bid one spade on a four-card suit even though you had longer clubs or diamonds, e.g.

♠ J 10 9 4
♡ A 6
◇ 7
♣ Q 6 5 4 3 2

15

With no four-card suit which can be shown at the one level, you may bid 1NT even with a hand that is not really flat, e.g.

♠ Q 7 3
♡ A 6
♢ 7 5
♣ 9 8 6 4 3 2

In this awkward situation you are really making the least bad bid rather than necessarily the one you might have ideally liked to make. It may look awkward, but experience has shown that this scheme really does work better than any of the alternatives, and the problems are much less serious in practice than they may appear at first sight.

QUIZ TWO
The First Response

Partner opens one.club, what should you respond?

1) ♠ 8 3
   ♡ A 5 2
   ◇ K 6 4 3
   ♣ 10 9 6 4

2) ♠ 7 2
   ♡ A K 3
   ◇ J 7 6 4
   ♣ K 10 9 3

3) ♠ A J 7 6
   ♡ 7 4
   ◇ J 9 3
   ♣ Q 6 4 2

4) ♠ Q 10 8 7 4
   ♡ A J 6 3 2
   ◇ 5 2
   ♣ 7

5) ♠ A J 10 4
   ♡ Q J 7 6
   ◇ 8 3 2
   ♣ 7 4

6) ♠ K J 3
   ♡ Q 10 4
   ◇ Q 6 3 2
   ♣ J 3 2

7) ♠ A J 3
   ♡ K 10 4
   ◇ K J 6 3
   ♣ Q 7 5

8) ♠ A Q J 2
   ♡ A K 7 4 2
   ◇ 7 6
   ♣ 8 3

Partner opens one heart, what do you respond?

9) ♠ K763
♡ QJ42
◇ 763
♣ Q2

10) ♠ QJ4
♡ KJ63
◇ 7
♣ A10642

11) ♠ K874
♡ QJ2
◇ 9632
♣ K5

12) ♠ QJ3
♡ K64
◇ Q732
♣ A104

13) ♠ K75
♡ 64
◇ AJ1075
♣ K32

14) ♠ J1063
♡ 97
◇ AJ1062
♣ J3

15) ♠ J103
♡ 94
◇ AJ6432
♣ 105

16) ♠ Q107
♡ K643
◇ A97
♣ QJ9

17) ♠ Q107
♡ J432
◇ 1097
♣ J84

SOLUTIONS TO QUIZ TWO

The First Response

Partner opens one diamond. What do you respond?

1) ♠ 83
    ♡ A 5 2
    ◇ K 6 4 3
    ♣ 10 9 6 4

Two clubs. You have four cards in partner's suit and have no reason to think that a suit other than clubs should be trumps. The single raise shows 6–9 points and at least four clubs.

2) ♠ 72
    ♡ A K 3
    ◇ J 7 6 4
    ♣ K 10 9 3

Three clubs. This time you are too strong just to raise to two. Remember, always bid to the full value of your hand when supporting partner. In this case three clubs shows club support and 10–12 points.

3) ♠ A J 7 6
    ♡ 74
    ◇ J 9 3
    ♣ Q 6 4 2

One spade. With four clubs you could support partner, however it is better to look for a major-suit fit first. You will always get a second chance as your change of suit forces partner to bid again, so if he doesn't like spades you can go back to clubs next time.

4) ♠ Q 10 8 7 4
    ♡ A J 6 3 2
    ◇ 5 2
    ♣ 7

One spade. The higher of two five-card suits. Why? Suppose partner's rebid is two clubs or 1NT, won't you want to bid your second suit next to give him a choice? 1♣ – 1♠ – 1NT – 2♡ enables him to choose either one while remaining at the two-level, 1♣ – 1♡ – 1NT – 2♠ does not. That is why you bid the higher suit first, so as to prepare for your second bid.

5) ♠ A J 10 4
    ♡ Q J 7 6
    ◇ 8 3 2
    ♣ 7 4

One heart. Fairly balanced, but a four-card major at the one level is always preferable to 1NT. With two four-card suits bid the lower one first. After 1♣ – 1♡ partner can bid one spade, if he has four, if not you can forget about them as an eight-card fit is impossible. After 1♣ – 1♠ on the other hand it may not be convenient for him to bid two hearts with four hearts, as that would push the bidding higher.

6) ♠ K J 3
   ♡ Q 10 4
   ◊ Q 6 3 2
   ♣ J 3 2

1NT. Perfectly flat, and the only four-card suit is a minor so there is no reason not to bid 1NT, which shows 6–9 HCPs. There is nothing wrong with one diamond, it just gives less information.

7) ♠ A J 3
   ♡ K 10 4
   ◊ K J 6 3
   ♣ Q 7 5

3NT. Again, a completely flat hand, so no-trumps looks the spot. As always when bidding no-trumps you should bid the full limit of your hand straight -away. With 14 HCPs facing an opening hand you *know* you have enough between you for game, so you must bid it.

8) ♠ A Q J 2
   ♡ A K 7 4 2
   ◊ 7 6
   ♣ 8 3

One heart. Your longest suit. Remember, one heart is forcing, i.e. partner must bid again, so there is no need to jump. Until a trump fit is found, you need to conserve as much bidding space as possible. After a fit is found, *then* you can jump.

9) ♠ K 7 6 3
   ♡ Q J 4 2
   ◊ 7 6 3
   ♣ Q 2

Two hearts. With four-card support for partner's major suit there is no need to look elsewhere.

10) ♠ Q J 4
    ♡ K J 6 3
    ◊ 7
    ♣ A 10 6 4 2

Four hearts. You already know there are sufficient hearts between the two hands so, even with a longer club suit, should not complicate the issue by changing the suit. Including the extra points for the singleton diamond you have 14, enough to expect to make game and, as always, you must therefore bid it immediately.

11) ♠ K 8 7 4
    ♡ Q J 2
    ◊ 9 6 3 2
    ♣ K 5

One spade. Flattish, but a four-card major at the one level always takes precedence over 1NT.

12) ♠ Q J 3
    ♡ K 6 4
    ◊ Q 7 3 2
    ♣ A 10 4

2NT. ... but a four-card minor at the two level does not take precedence over 2NT. With a flat hand make the appropriate limit bid to show your strength.

20

13) ♠ K75
   ♡ 64
   ♢ AJ1075
   ♣ K32

Two diamonds. 11 HCPs and a five-card suit, what else?

14) ♠ J1063
   ♡ 97
   ♢ AJ1062
   ♣ J3

One spade. With only 7 HCPs you cannot go to the two level, much as you would like to bid diamonds. Fortunately you have a reasonable alternative, the new suit at the one level only promises 6 HCPs.

15) ♠ J103
   ♡ 94
   ♢ AJ6432
   ♣ 105

1NT. Again you are too weak to bid two diamonds, but this time you have only three spades so you cannot bid those either. The only thing left is 1NT. While you try to have a flat hand, the 1NT response also has to take in awkward hands like this one which just don't fit in anywhere else.

16) ♠ Q107
   ♡ K643
   ♢ A97
   ♣ QJ9

Three hearts. Yes, you are completely balanced and might be tempted to bid no-trumps, but you also have four-card support for partner's major suit and must say so. After all, partner may not be as balanced as you are, so hearts will almost certainly be the right contract.

17) ♠ Q107
   ♡ J432
   ♢ 1097
   ♣ J84

Pass. Despite the four-card heart support you have to pass, as you simply do not have the 6 HCPs required to make a response.

One of a Suit — Opener's rebid

Responder made a limit bid

Things are relatively straightforward when responder has made a limit bid, as you know almost everything there is to know about his hand immediately. Firstly, suppose that he has supported your suit. Usually, you can be confident that this suit should be trumps and the only remaining question is how high to go — which can be answered simply by adding points together. For example:

West	East
1♡	2♡
?	

The two heart bid shows roughly 6–9 points, and we know that about 26 points are needed between the two hands to make four hearts a reasonable proposition, so opener should now bid as follows:

With up to 16 points, for example:

♠ A 6
♡ A Q J 7 6
♢ K 3 2
♣ 9 6 4

Pass, as there cannot be 26 points between the two hands.

With 19 plus points, for example:

♠ A 6
♡ A Q J 7 6
♢ K 3 2
♣ K Q 4

Bid four hearts, as there will usually be 26 points between the two hands.

With 17 or 18 points, for example:

♠ A 6
♡ A Q J 7 6
♢ K 3 2
♣ K 6 4

You will not know whether there are the points for game. Opposite six points a part-score will be sufficient, but if partner has nine points you should try a game contract. The correct bid is three hearts, saying to partner "I know that you have 6–9 points but am unsure whether or not to bid game. With a minimum response (6–7 points) please pass, but with a maximum (8–9) please bid game". Remember that two hearts plus one scores the same as three hearts, so there would be no reason for opener to bid on unless he had interest in greater things.

West   **East**
1♡   3♡
?

This time responder has shown a better hand, 10–12 points, so opener needs correspondingly less to have an interest in game. With a minimum opening, up to 14 points, he should pass, as the three heart bid tells him that this is the limit of the hand, unless *he* has something to spare. With a little extra, 15 plus, he bids the game.

West   **East**
1♡   4♡
?

Responder has shown 13–15 points, but opener will rarely bid again as four hearts is already game. The only time he will bid again is when he has such a powerful hand, 18 plus points, that he thinks there may be a chance of a slam and the rich bonus which comes with contracting for and making twelve tricks — roughly double the score for a game contract. For example:

♠ A Q J 4
♡ K Q J 10 7
♢ A J 10
♣ 5

We will look at how to explore slam possibilities in a later section of this book. ♭ ♭ ♯

In all the above cases the point count given is the total point count including not only high cards but also the extra points allowed for distribution.

Now let us look at what happens when responder's first bid was in no-trumps. Again, he has made a limit bid describing both the strength and shape of his hand. Things are not quite as simple, however, as it is not yet certain what suit, if any, should be trumps. If opener also has a balanced hand then no-trumps should suffice, if he has a very long suit he will want it to be trumps, while with two long suits he may wish responder to choose between them. This gives us the following scheme.

Opener is also balanced

After 1♡ – 1NT, the opener holds:

15–16 HCPs	—	Pass as there cannot be sufficient for game.
17–18 HCP	—	2NT; there may or may not be the points required. so invite game.
19+ HCPs	—	3NT; there must be sufficient for game.

After 1♡ – 1NT – 2NT, responder passes with a minimum, for example:

♠ K 6 3
♡ 7 4 2
◇ J 7 3
♣ Q 8 4 2

but bids 3NT with a maximum, e.g.

♠ A 6 3
♡ 7 4 2
◇ K 7 3
♣ Q 8 4 2

1♡ – 1NT showed only 6–9 HCPs so opener needed quite a strong hand to make a move towards game. After 1♡ – 2NT, however, he only needs a little over a minimum opening as responder has shown 11–12 HCPs. Opener should pass 2NT with 12–13, but raise to game with 14 or more.

1♡ – 3NT shows 13–15 HCPs but 3NT is already game so opener will rarely bid again with a flat hand. If he does he must be interested in a slam. With 19+ HCPs he could raise to 4NT to invite partner to bid a slam with a maximum hand.

Opener is unbalanced

West	East
1♡	1NT
2♡	

This shows a long suit but no interest in game. For example:

♠ A 6
♡ K J 9 7 6 4
◇ Q 3 2
♣ K 4

Responder is expected to pass.

West	East
1♡	1NT
3♡	

This shows a long suit (six plus cards) and invites game. For example:

♠ A Q 3
♡ A Q J 7 6 3
◇ A 10 2
♣ 6

Responder may pass with a minimum but should bid 3NT or four hearts with a maximum. Remember that if opener has a good six-card suit then responder needs very little support to make it a satisfactory trump suit.

West	East
1♡	1NT
4♡	

This is to play. It shows a long suit which you are sure should be trumps even if partner has no support for it and a strong game-going hand. For example:

♠ A K
♡ K Q 10 8 7 4 3
◇ Q J 10
♣ 4

Responder must pass.

West	East
1♡	2NT
3♡	

This shows a long suit but a weak hand. Responder should pass, but may occasionally raise with a nice looking maximum such as:

♠ A 6
♡ K 3 2
◇ A J 10 2
♣ 7 6 4 3

West	East
1♡	2NT
4♡	

This is to play with a long suit and extra values. Responder must pass.

West	East
1♡	3NT
4♡	

Opener has a long suit and thinks that four hearts will be safer than 3NT. Responder must pass.

When opener has a second suit, things again get a little more complicated.

West	East
1♡	1NT
2♣/♢	

This shows five hearts and a second suit of at least four cards, for example:

♠ A 6
♡ A J 10 7 4
♢ K J 3 2
♣ 7 4

Responder is expected to choose between the two suits, either by passing or by going back to two hearts.

Opener is not strong enough to insist on game, but just in case he has quite a good hand, responder may occasionally raise the second suit with a good fit and a maximum. For example:

♠ 7 4
♡ K 6
♢ J 9 3 2
♣ A 8 7 5 4

West	East
1♡	1NT
3♣/♢	

This shows a second suit and a strong hand, for example:

♠ A K
♡ A Q J 7 4
♢ A J 3 2
♣ 7 4

Responder must bid again, and may support either suit or go back to 3NT. When supporting one of opener's suits, he may go back to the first suit with only three cards, as opener will always have

26

five to bid this way, but must have four to raise the second suit as opener will often only have four himself.

West   **East**
1♡   2NT
3♣/◇

This shows a second suit and forces responder to bid again. He may support the first suit with three, the second with four, or revert to no-trumps.

West   **East**
1♡   3NT
4♣/◇

This shows a second suit and forces responder to bid again. To go beyond 3NT, which is already game, opener must be strong enough to be prepared to go to the five level if partner prefers his second suit, so he must have a good hand. Often, he will be at least considering the possibility of a slam. Responder should usually choose one of opener's suits, and only revert to no-trumps with almost all his high cards in partner's short suits. For example, bid 1♠ – 3NT – 4◇ – 4NT on:

♠ 10 6
♡ A Q J 4
◇ Q 9 3
♣ K Q 10 2

To bid a second suit opener will always be at least 5-4, as with two four-card suits he would have a fairly balanced hand and would be happy to stay in no-trumps. Although opener may prove to have five cards in both suits, his first suit will often prove to be longer than the second. With no preference between them responder should therefore always go back to the first suit rather than just pass the second one out. For example, bid 1♡ – 1NT – 2◇ – 2♡ with:

♠ K 6 3
♡ 10 6 3
◇ 10 6 3
♣ A 9 6 4

Bidding a second time in this way does not suggest any extra strength, merely that you think this is the better suit to have as trumps.

Responder bids a new suit — i.e. a non-limit bid

When the first response is in a new suit, opener must bid again, as responder could have many different types of hand and may need a second chance to describe his actual holding. With his rebid, opener must try to describe both the shape and strength of his own hand, always adding something to the information already given. To describe his shape, he should show the most important feature of his hand that partner does not yet know about. In other words, there is no point in giving the same message twice. If you have already bid a suit once to say this is my longest suit and I have at least four of them, it would be silly to repeat the same suit unless you have more than four cards in it. That would just be repeating the original message. To bid the same suit twice you must have at least five, three times six and so on, so that each time you bid it you are telling partner something new. This restriction, as we have already seen, does not apply, of course, if partner has supported your suit thereby setting it as trumps.

1) With four cards in responder's suit opener should support it, and in so doing he should bid the full limit of his hand. In other words, the stronger his hand the higher the level to which he should raise the suit, just as he would if he were supporting opener's suit. As usual when making a limit bid, opener should assume that partner has a minimum hand, six plus for a one-level response or nine plus for a two-level response, until proven otherwise.

For example, after 1♢ – 1♠:

Rebid two spades with 13–15 points, a minimum opening, e.g.:

♠ Q 7 4 2
♡ A 6
♢ A J 10 9 7
♣ J 6

Rebid three spades with 16–18 points to strongly invite game, e.g.

♠ A Q 4 2
♡ A 6
♢ A J 10 9 7
♣ J 6

Rebid four spades with 19 plus points as there must be enough for game between the two hands, e.g.

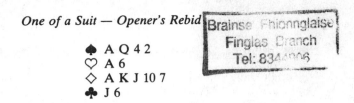

```
♠ A Q 4 2
♡ A 6
♢ A K J 10 7
♣ J 6
```

Because there is a known trump fit opener may add distributional points if he has a shortage in a side suit, and these are included in the above totals.

2)   With a balanced hand — 4-3-3-3, 4-4-3-2, 5-3-3-2 — and less than four cards in partner's suit, bid no-trumps. Again, opener must show his strength by the level at which he bids. He cannot have 12–14 HCPs as he would then have opened 1NT, so the scheme is as follows:

After a one-level response, for example after 1♢ – 1♠:

1NT shows 15–16 HCPs
2NT shows 17–18 HCPs
3NT shows 19 plus HCPs

After a two-level response, for example after 1♡ – 2♣:

2NT shows 15–16 HCPs
3NT shows 17 plus HCPs

All these are limit bids, in other words they do not force partner to speak again.

3)   With a six-card suit, or a strong five-carder, rebid it. After a one-level response such as 1♢ – 1♠ bid two diamonds with 12–15 points, three diamonds with 16 plus. Neither of these rebids is forcing, but obviously three diamonds is very encouraging. After a two-level response such as 1♡ – 2♣, bid two hearts with 12–15, three hearts with 16 plus. Two hearts is not forcing as responder may be able to see immediately that there are not the points for game, but three hearts is, as with 16 plus facing nine plus there must be a minimum of 25 points between the two hands and game should be reached. So with:

```
♠ A 5          Bid  1♢–1♠–2♢
♡ Q 3          or   1♢–2♣–2♢.
♢ K J 9 7 3 2
♣ Q 6 3
```

But with:

29

♠ A 5   Bid 1♢ – 1♠ – 3♢
♡ A Q   or   1♢ – 2♣ – 3♢.
♢ K J 9 7 3 2
♣ Q 6 3

4) Bid a second four- or five-card suit. Where possible it is better to bid a second suit, thereby giving partner a choice, rather than repeat your original five-card suit. When you bid two suits partner will usually take you to have five of the first anyway, so you will be giving him an extra piece of information by bidding a new suit.

There is, however, a slight complication to consider. Where the second suit can be bid *below* the next level of the first suit, e.g. 1♡ – 2♣ – 2♢, or 1♣ – 1♡ – 1♠, there is no problem and the second suit should always be shown as the rebid. Where the second suit would have to be shown by a bid *above* a rebid of the first suit, e.g. 1♡ – 2♣ – 2♠, or 1♣ – 1♡ – 2♢, the effect of the rebid is to push the bidding higher.

Look at the difference. Responder, with just a minimum hand for his first bid, will usually just want to choose between opener's suits as cheaply as possible. After 1♡ – 2♣ – 2♢, he can choose either suit at the two level, either by passing or by going back to two hearts. After 1♡ – 2♣ – 2♠, he has to go up to the three level to go back to the first suit (three hearts), for example, with:

♠ Q 6
♡ Q 6 3
♢ 8 7 5
♣ A J 10 9 7

If the bidding is pushed higher, it means that at the end of the day you are going to have to make more tricks and will need more high cards between you with which to make them. It makes sense that, whenever a player does push the bidding higher, he should have the extra strength which will be needed in the play. The rule is that, if a player bids two suits in such an order that if partner wants to go back to the first suit he has to go to the three level to do so, then he promises at least 16 points in his hand. Bidding two suits in this way is called "reversing". If you do not have 16 plus points you cannot reverse and must content yourself with simply repeating your first suit. For example, after 1♡ – 2♣, bid two spades with:

♠ A Q 5 4
♡ K J 10 7 3
♢ A K
♣ 7 5

But two hearts with:

♠ A Q 5 4
♡ K J 10 7 3
♢ K 5
♣ 7 5

Note that you are still following the basic rule on which suit to open –
longer. A reverse always guarantees more cards in the first suit than the se
With 5-5 you open the higher, and with 4-4 the lower, but then rebid no-tru
You do not reverse just to show strength, you are also showing distributio

As we shall see later, after a one-level response a reverse forces partne
bid just once more, whilst after a two-level response the bidding must
kept open, until game is reached. The reason for the difference is that aft
a two-level response you are known to have at least 16 points opposite a
least nine, a minimum of 25 between the two hands — enough for game
After a one-level response there may only be 16 opposite six, not enough
for game, unless someone has a bit to spare.

There is another way for opener to show a strong hand, and that is to jump
in his second suit. A jump such as 1♡ – 1♠ – 3♣ or 1♠ – 2♣ – 3♡ is
forcing all the way to game. After a one-level response opener needs getting
on for 19 points to be sure of game; after a two-level response, where
responder has promised a little more, he needs only 16 plus. With any less,
opener should just change the suit without jumping.

To summarise:

1♣ – 1♡ – 1♠	is not forcing and neither promises nor denies extra values.
1♣ – 1♡ – 2♠	is forcing to game, 19 plus points.
1♡ – 1♠ – 2♣	is not forcing and neither promises nor denies extra values.
1♡ – 1♠ – 3♣	is forcing to game, 19 plus points.
1♣ – 1♠ – 2♡	is forcing for one round, 16 plus points.
1♠ – 2♣ – 2♡	is not forcing and shows 12–15 points.
1♠ – 2♣ – 3♡	is forcing to game, 16 plus points.
1♡ – 2♣ – 2♠	is forcing to game, 16 plus points. If you reverse there is no need to jump to show a big hand.
1♠ – 2♡ – 3♣	is forcing to game, 16 plus points.

Rather than simply trying to memorise the above table, try to work out why
each bid means what it does. If in the future you do forget one, you will
then be able to work it out from first principles. Obviously, the above are
only examples, other equivalent sequences — ones which have the same
effect but involve different suits — have the same meanings as the ones listed.

QUIZ THREE

Opener's Rebid

In each case, what should opener rebid?

			West	East
1)	♠ K J 5 3 ♡ A Q 7 4 2 ♢ 7 ♣ Q 6 2		West 1♡ ?	East 1♠
2)	♠ A 1 0 8 7 ♡ K 6 ♢ A K Q 6 2 ♣ 7 4		West 1♢ ?	East 1♠
3)	♠ K 7 2 ♡ A Q J 7 ♢ K 6 3 ♣ Q J 2		West 1♡ ?	East 1♠
4)	♠ A Q 3 ♡ A J ♢ Q 7 3 ♣ K J 1 0 6 4		West 1♣ ?	East 1♡
5)	♠ A Q J ♡ A J 7 4 2 ♢ K J 5 ♣ Q 3		West 1♡ ?	East 2♣
6)	♠ 7 2 ♡ A Q J ♢ K 3 ♣ A Q 1 0 9 6 4		West 1♣ ?	East 1♢
7)	♠ Q 7 ♡ A J 1 0 6 4 2 ♢ K 7 ♣ Q 6 3		West 1♡ ?	East 2♣

8)
♠ 86
♡ A Q J 4 2
♢ K J 7 3
♣ Q 2

West	East
1♡	2♣
?	

9)
♠ K J 10 3
♡ A Q J 5 2
♢ Q 7
♣ 6 2

West	East
1♡	2♣
?	

10)
♠ K J 10 3
♡ A Q J 5 2
♢ A 7
♣ Q 3

West	East
1♡	2♣
?	

11)
♠ K 3
♡ A Q 10 6 4
♢ 8 5
♣ A 10 7 3

West	East
1♡	2♣
?	

12)
♠ K 10 7 2
♡ A 3
♢ 10 5
♣ A Q J 6 4

West	East
1♣	1♡
?	

13)
♠ A K 6 2
♡ A Q 2
♢ 7
♣ A Q 10 7 2

West	East
1♣	1♡
?	

14)
♠ 7 3
♡ Q 2
♢ A Q 7 2
♣ A J 10 6 3

West	East
1♣	1♡
?	

15)
♠ A K 10 7 3
♡ Q 4
♢ Q 3
♣ A Q 6 4

West	East
1♠	2♡
?	

16)
♠ A K 10 7 3
♡ A Q J 6 4
♢ K 5
♣ 7

West	East
1♠	2♣
?	

SOLUTIONS TO QUIZ THREE
Opener's Rebid

1)	♠ K J 5 3	West	East
	♡ A Q 7 4 2	1♡	1♠
	♢ 7	?	
	♣ Q 6 2		

Two spades. When you can support your partner's major suit this should always be your first priority. As you have only a bare minimum opening, you do so as cheaply as possible.

2)	♠ A 10 8 7	West	East
	♡ K 6	1♢	1♠
	♢ A K Q 6 2	?	
	♣ 7 4		

Three spades. Again, with four cards in partner's suit and therefore at least eight between the two hands, you should support him. This time, however, though you do not have sufficient to guarantee game, you do have more than just a bare opener. Three spades tells partner this, saying that you have about 16–18 points and inviting him to bid game if he has a little to spare for his initial response.

3)	♠ K 7 2	West	East
	♡ A Q J 7	1♡	1♠
	♢ K 6 3	?	
	♣ Q J 2		

1NT. The only reason you didn't open your balanced hand with 1NT was because you were too strong to do so. Rebidding 1NT says exactly that, showing a balanced hand with 15–16 HCPs.

4)	♠ A Q 3	West	East
	♡ A J	1♣	1♡
	◇ Q 7 3	?	
	♣ K J 10 6 4		

2NT. Though you have a five-card suit, you have already bid it once and your hand is essentially balanced. This is the main feature that partner does not yet know about. 1NT would show the shape but not the strength, with 17 or 18 points 2NT is the correct limit bid.

5)	♠ A Q J	West	East
	♡ A J 7 4 2	1♡	2♣
	◇ K J 5	?	
	♣ Q 3		

3NT. Once again you have a five-card suit, but with no really weak suit this is a no-trump hand. After a two-level response 2NT would show only 15–16 points, so here you must jump to game, showing 17 plus. After all, you know there are a minimum of 27 points between the two hands, so you must get to game ever.tually.

6)	♠ 7 2	West	East
	♡ A Q J	1♣	1◇
	◇ K 3	?	
	♣ A Q 10 9 6 4		

Three clubs. The extra club length is the main thing to tell partner about, but you must also jump to show your extra strength. Even if the ace of hearts were taken away you would still have an opening bid, so with an ace to spare you should give partner the good news.

7)	♠ Q 7	West	East
	♡ A J 10 6 4 2	1♡	2♣
	◇ K 7	?	
	♣ Q 6 3		

Two hearts. A minimum hand but a good long suit. What else would you bid?

		West	East
8)	♠ 86	West	East
	♡ A Q J 4 2	1♡	2♣
	◇ K J 7 3	?	
	♣ Q 2		

Two diamonds. With 5-4 in two suits, always give partner a choice if you can. A two heart rebid would show the fifth heart but say nothing about diamonds, whereas a two diamond rebid tells about the diamonds but also virtually guarantees five hearts. Why? Because with two four-card suits you would have opened one diamond, the lower one, wouldn't you?

		West	East
9)	♠ K J 10 3	West	East
	♡ A Q J 5 2	1♡	2♣
	◇ Q 7	?	
	♣ 6 2		

Two hearts. You cannot show the second suit because two spades would be a reverse, forcing the bidding to the three level and so showing a strong hand. With a minimum opening you cannot afford to do that, so you must content yourself with rebidding your five-card suit.

		West	East
10)	♠ K J 10 3	West	East
	♡ A Q J 5 2	1♡	2♣
	◇ A 7	?	
	♣ Q 3		

Two spades. Now you do have the extra strength required so can afford to show your second suit. No need to jump, the reverse shows a strong hand and compels partner to bid again.

		West	East
11)	♠ K 3	West	East
	♡ A Q 10 6 4	1♡	2♣
	◇ 8 5	?	
	♣ A 10 7 3		

Three clubs. With four-card support you must raise partner's suit, and as your hand is minimum you do so as cheaply as possible.

12)	♠ K 10 7 2		**West**	**East**
	♡ A 3		1♣	1♡
	◇ 10 5		?	
	♣ A Q J 6 4			

One spade. With 5-4 bid the second suit if you can. This is not a reverse; one spade is actually cheaper than a repeat of your first suit, as it does not push the bidding up.

13)	♠ A K 6 2		**West**	**East**
	♡ A Q 2		1♣	1♡
	◇ 7		?	
	♣ A Q 10 7 2			

Two spades. Again, you show your second suit, but with such a powerful hand you want to reach game eventually, so must jump to force partner to keep bidding.

14)	♠ 7 3		**West**	**East**
	♡ Q 2		1♣	1♡
	◇ A Q 7 2		?	
	♣ A J 10 6 3			

Two clubs. Two diamonds would unfortunately be a reverse and with your minimum hand you are not strong enough for that, so must just repeat your first suit.

15)	♠ A K 10 7 3		**West**	**East**
	♡ Q 4		1♠	2♡
	◇ Q 3		?	
	♣ A Q 6 4			

Three clubs. This is a high-level reverse and shows 16 plus points without the need to jump. Partner will know that there are the points for game, so he will obviously bid again.

16)	♠ A K 10 7 3		**West**	**East**
	♡ A Q J 6 4		1♠	2♣
	◇ K 5		?	
	♣ 7			

Three hearts. You must show your second suit, but two hearts would only show about 12–15 points and would not be forcing. Opposite a two-level response you want to be in game, so you must jump to give partner the good news and compel him to keep bidding.

The Auction Continues

As opener has already made two bids, a good deal is now known about his hand, particularly with regard to the distribution, and responder will frequently be in a position to decide on the final contract. Just what his options actually are, will depend on what has happened in the auction so far.

One player has made a limit bid

If your first response was a limit bid, i.e. you either raised partner's suit or bid no-trumps, you will have already described your hand pretty well and should only bid again if invited to do so. For example, 1♡ – 1NT – 2♡ does not give you an option, partner already knows that you have 6–9 points and could not support hearts, yet he still wants hearts to be trumps. However much you may dislike hearts, you must not bid again, as partner has made the final decision. On the other hand, after 1♡ – 1NT – 2♣, you may bid again. This time you have been asked to choose between two suits. Your options are to bid two hearts with hearts equal to or longer than clubs, pass with longer clubs, or raise to three clubs with a maximum and four or more clubs. Occasionally you might also bid a six-card diamond suit, if neither clubs nor hearts appeal to you, e.g.

> ♠ Q 3 2
> ♡ 7 6
> ◇ K J 9 8 7 5
> ♣ 8 3

If partner has bid a game contract, you must pass unless he has given you a choice of contracts. 1♡ – 2♡ – 3NT would show a powerful balanced hand with only four hearts and ask you to decide between 3NT and four hearts, e.g.

> ♠ A J 3
> ♡ A 10 6 2
> ◇ K Q 9
> ♣ A J 10

while 1♠ – 3NT – 4♡ would show a two-suited hand and ask you to pass or return to four spades, e.g.

♠ A Q 7 4 2
♡ A J 9 6 3
◇ J 6
♣ 3

1♡ – 2♡ – 4♡ or 1♡ – 1NT – 3NT does not offer a choice and you should pass automatically. The difference is that the latter two examples see both players bidding the same "suit" in a way which suggests that that suit should clearly be trumps. Partner knows how strong you are and has decided how high to go, so there are no further decisions to be made. On the other hand, what about 1♡ – 2♡ – 3♡, or 1♡ – 1NT – 2NT? Again, you are both bidding the same "suit". As three hearts scores exactly the same as two hearts plus one, why has partner not just passed and avoided the risk of going down in three hearts? The only answer that makes sense is that he is still interested in higher things — game — but is unable to bid it himself. He knows you have 6–9 points, so presumably 8 or 9 would make game a fair bet while 6 or 7 would not, and only you know which you actually have. Where game has not yet been reached, you may bid again, even though you have both bid the same suit, because partner may, as here, be inviting you to bid game if you are maximum.

The only time responder is forced to bid again is if partner jumps in a new suit or makes a strength showing reverse. For example, 1♡ – 1NT – 3♣, or 1♡ – 1NT – 2♠, where partner has forced the bidding to a high level specifically to show a strong hand. He is interested in game and wants you to express a preference between his two suits, though in this case you are also permitted to return to no-trumps if you prefer. For example, after 1♡ – 1NT – 3♣, suppose you hold:

♠ A64	♠ A6	♠ KJ4
♡ J73	♡ J7	♡ 73
◇ Q632	◇ 76542	◇ K10863
♣ 742	♣ Q986	♣ 652
Bid three hearts	Bid four clubs	Bid 3NT

Opener's rebid was a limit bid

There are two ways in which opener can make a limit bid at his second turn. Firstly, he can support whatever you bid, e.g. 1♡ – 1♠ – 3♠ or 1♡ – 1NT – 2NT. As you have agreed what trumps should be, if any, the only remaining question is how high to go. Partner's limit bid has told you the strength of his hand, so it is a simple matter of adding your points to his and deciding how high to go. If there are insufficient points for game, you should pass, as there is no point in getting any higher. If you are unsure you may be able to ask partner to decide, e.g. 1♡ – 1♠ – 2♠ – 3♠ asks partner to bid four spades with a maximum two spade bid, but to pass with a minimum. If you can see that there is enough for game you must, of course, bid it immediately as always.

The second way in which opener can make a limit rebid is by bidding no-trumps at his second turn. Again, you will know exactly how strong he is, you know his longest suit, and you know that he is fairly balanced, so you are well placed to pick the final contract. If you are happy with no-trumps you can either pass or raise as is appropriate, simply add points together to decide. With a long suit you can rebid it, safe in the knowledge that partner must hold at least two. With a weak hand bid as cheaply as possible, e.g. bid 1♡ – 1♠ – 1NT – 2♠ on:

> ♠ Q J 7 6 3 2
> ♡ 9 4
> ♢ K 7 3
> ♣ 8 6

and partner will let you play there. With a strong hand jump to game in the suit.

Finally you may have a second suit and want to give partner a choice. As usual, a simple bid is weak, e.g. 1♡ – 1♠ – 1NT – 2♣, only allowing partner to bid two spades or pass, while a jump, 1♡ – 1♠ – 1NT – 3♣, is strong and forces partner to bid again.

Opener rebids his original suit

If opener rebids his first suit as cheaply as possible, e.g. 1♡ – 1♠ – 2♡, he is showing a long suit but a minimum opening — up to about 15 points. With a weak hand responder is usually best to pass even if he does not like opener's suit. He has shown a long suit, and to insist on playing other than in that suit merely risks getting higher with no guarantee of improving matters. If you have two long suits, at least five cards each, *and* can give partner a choice without raising the level you may do so, otherwise just keep your fingers crossed and pass. So, 1♣ – 1♠ – 2♣ – 2♡ with:

> ♠ K J 10 6 4
> ♡ K 9 8 7 3
> ♢ 6 4
> ♣ 2

where partner can pass or bid two spades is OK, but 1♣ – 1♡ – 2♣ – 2♠ with:

♠ K J 7 3
♡ K J 10 6 4
♢ 8 6 3
♣ 2

where partner might have to go up to three hearts, is not. As always when the level of bidding has been raised, the latter sequence shows a strong hand.

With a good hand you can, and of course must, bid for a second time. You may support partner's suit even with three small cards as he is now known to have at least five. With stoppers in both unbid suits you can bid no-trumps. In either of these cases you should bid the full limit of your hand — bid 2NT or raise to three of partner's suit with about 11 or 12 points, bid game with more. Finally, you may bid a new suit. If this is a jump, a reverse, or at the three level, it is a strong and forcing bid. So: 1♡ – 1♠ – 2♡ – 3♣, 1♡ – 2♢ – 2♡ – 2♠ and 1♣ – 1♠ – 2♣ – 3♡ are all strong bids because they raise the level, but 1♣ – 1♠ – 2♣ – 2♡ is weak because it does not.

⋅ Where opener's rebid was a jump, e.g. 1♡ – 1♠ – 3♡, he has shown roughly 16–18 points and you should strain to bid again if you possibly can, but with a bare minimum hand you may occasionally pass. After a two-level response, a jump rebid is forcing to game. Usually you will be choosing between raising partner's suit and bidding no-trumps. Remember that he has promised a good six-card suit so you can support with a doubleton. You may, however, bid your own suit again or a new suit if it is a long one.

Opener has bid two suits

With a weak hand, responder should choose between partner's suits, always remembering that if they are of unequal length he will have bid the longer one first. Alternatively, responder may rebid his own suit if he can do so without raising the level *and* it is of at least six cards in length. He may also bid 1NT with the unbid suit covered if he does not like either of opener's suits, e.g. 1♣ – 1♢ – 1♠ – 1NT on:

♠ 6 4 3
♡ K Q 3
♢ Q 10 7 5 2
♣ J 2

With a reasonable hand, about 10–12 points, responder will still be interested in game but unable to guarantee it. He should make a limit bid, inviting opener to go on if he is maximum. For example, 1♡ – 1♠ – 2◇ – 2NT shows about 10–12 points with no great liking for partner's suits but the clubs well stopped, while 1♡ – 1♠ – 2♣ – 3♡ shows three-card heart support and 10–12 points. You can afford to do this with only three because partner will normally have five cards in his first suit when he bids two suits like this. Responder may also rebid his own suit if it is a six-carder and is strong, but this time he must jump to invite game, e.g. 1♡ – 1♠ – 2♣ – 3♠. With 13 plus points responder should want to get to game, so should jump all the way to game if bidding no-trumps or supporting partner, while if unsure of where to go he may bid the fourth suit to elicit further information from opener. This last is a more advanced idea which will be discussed later.

If opener's second suit was a jump, then he has shown a hand which wants to play in game, so responder must bid again. As always, if he knows where he wants to go he should just bid the appropriate game, while if he is unsure he should make a bid which tells opener more about his shape and let him decide.

QUIZ FOUR
The Auction Continues

In each case, what is your next bid?

		West	East
1)	♠ A 3 ♡ Q 10 4 2 ◇ Q 7 4 ♣ 8 6 5 2	1♡ 3♡	2♡ ?
2)	♠ Q 6 4 ♡ 7 ◇ A J 9 7 6 ♣ J 8 6 4	1♡ 2♡	1NT ?
3)	♠ A 6 3 ♡ Q 6 ◇ K 7 5 3 ♣ 8 6 4 3	1♡ 2◇	1NT ?
4)	♠ 7 4 2 ♡ J 6 ◇ Q J 4 2 ♣ Q 10 7 4	1♡ 2NT	1NT ?
5)	♠ 7 2 ♡ Q 7 4 ◇ Q 8 7 3 2 ♣ K J 6	1♡ 3♣	1NT ?
6)	♠ Q 7 3 ♡ J 4 ◇ J 10 7 5 3 2 ♣ K 6	1♡ 3NT	1NT ?
7)	♠ 7 3 ♡ 10 5 ◇ Q 10 7 4 ♣ A Q J 6 3	1♠ 2♡	2♣ ?

			West	East
8)	♠ 104		**West**	**East**
	♡ J63		1♠	2♣
	◇ KJ4		3♡	?
	♣ AJ873			

9)	♠ Q103		**West**	**East**
	♡ 72		1♡	2♣
	◇ K104		2♡	?
	♣ AQ762			

10)	♠ 103		**West**	**East**
	♡ Q63		1♡	2♣
	◇ A104		2♡	?
	♣ AQJ62			

11)	♠ K72		**West**	**East**
	♡ 73		1♡	2♣
	◇ QJ2		2♠	?
	♣ QJ984			

12)	♠ 64		**West**	**East**
	♡ K73		1♡	2♣
	◇ A32		2NT	?
	♣ AJ1064			

13)	♠ KJ432		**West**	**East**
	♡ A7		1♡	1♠
	◇ A1042		2♣	?
	♣ 97			

14)	♠ Q108		**West**	**East**
	♡ 642		1♣	1◇
	◇ KJ873		1♠	?
	♣ 74			

15)	♠ KJ4		**West**	**East**
	♡ 72		1♡	2♣
	◇ KQ4		3♣	?
	♣ AJ732			

16) ♠ 73
   ♡ Q 3
   ♢ Q 1082
   ♣ A J 1064

West	East
1♡	2♣
3♡	?

17) ♠ K 1073
   ♡ 7
   ♢ Q 10864
   ♣ J 73

West	East
1♡	1♠
3♡	?

18) ♠ Q 1094
   ♡ K J 6
   ♢ K 10
   ♣ 10874

West	East
1♢	1♠
1NT	?

19) ♠ Q 86
   ♡ J 732
   ♢ K 93
   ♣ Q J 2

West	East
1♡	2♡
2NT	?

20) ♠ Q 732
   ♡ 86
   ♢ K J 732
   ♣ 104

West	East
1♣	1♢
2♠	?

SOLUTIONS TO QUIZ FOUR
The Auction Continues

1) ♠ A 3
    ♡ Q 10 4 2
    ◇ Q 7 4
    ♣ 8 6 5 2

West	East
1♡	2♡
3♡	?

Four hearts. Partner knows you have only 6–9 points, yet is still interested in game though unable to bid it himself. As you have a near maximum you should accept his invitation and raise to game.

2) ♠ Q 6 4
    ♡ 7
    ◇ A J 9 7 6
    ♣ J 8 6 4

West	East
1♡	1NT
2♡	?

Pass. However much you may dislike hearts, you cannot be sure that anything else will be any better. Partner has not offered you a choice, he has told you that he wants to play in two hearts.

3) ♠ A 6 3
    ♡ Q 6
    ◇ K 7 5 3
    ♣ 8 6 4 3

West	East
1♡	1NT
2◇	?

Three diamonds. As you prefer diamonds you could just pass, but with a nice maximum you should raise just in case partner might still be interested in game now that he has found support for one of his suits.

4) ♠ 7 4 2
    ♡ J 6
    ◇ Q J 4 2
    ♣ Q 10 7 4

West	East
1♡	1NT
2NT	?

Pass. Knowing that you have 6–9 points, partner has invited game. With a maximum (8–9) you would bid 3NT, but with your actual minimum you must pass.

5) ♠ 72   **West**   **East**
    ♡ Q74   1♡   1NT
    ◊ Q8732   3♣   ?
    ♣ KJ6

Four hearts. Partner's jump forces you to speak, but with a maximum and fitting cards in both his suits you are happy to do so. He must have at least five hearts so ♡Q74 is ample support. Give him the good news that you like hearts *and* are maximum by jumping to game.

6) ♠ Q73   **West**   **East**
    ♡ J4   1♡   1NT
    ◊ J107532   3NT   ?
    ♣ K6

Pass. No choice, partner has chosen the final contract and you have not been invited to the party.

7) ♠ 73   **West**   **East**
    ♡ 105   1♠   2♣
    ◊ Q1074   2♡   ?
    ♣ AQJ63

Two spades. You are not strong enough to raise the level of the bidding. 2NT looks the obvious bid, but that shows roughly the same 11–12 HCP it would have done had you bid it immediately, so it might persuade partner to raise you to a very poor game contract. All you can do is to choose between partner's suits, returning to the first one in case it is longer.

8) ♠ 104   **West**   **East**
    ♡ J63   1♠   2♣
    ◊ KJ4   3♡   ?
    ♣ AJ873

3NT. You must bid again because partner's jump tells you that he wants to play in game. Your preference is for hearts, but you cannot support a second suit with less than four cards. Fortunately, however, you have the unbid suit well stopped, so are in a position to bid 3NT.

9) ♠ Q 10 3
    ♡ 7 2
    ◇ K 10 4
    ♣ A Q 7 6 2

West	East
1♡	2♣
2♡	?

2NT. Partner's rebid showed a minimum opening hand, but he could still have as many as 14 or 15 points, in which case game could be on. You don't like hearts and have already shown your club suit, so bid 2NT to show your 11–12 HCP and invite game.

10) ♠ 10 3
    ♡ Q 6 3
    ◇ A 10 4
    ♣ A Q J 6 2

West	East
1♡	2♣
2♡	?

Four hearts. Now that partner has rebid his hearts you can support with three, and with 13 HCPs you have enough for game. Remember, when supporting partner's suit you must bid the full limit of your hand immediately.

11) ♠ K 7 2
    ♡ 7 3
    ◇ Q J 2
    ♣ Q J 9 8 4

West	East
1♡	2♣
2♠	?

2NT. Was your first thought to pass because you have a bare minimum two club bid and prefer spades to hearts? Partner has reversed, pushing the bidding up to the three-level had you preferred hearts, so he has a strong hand (16 plus) and wants to play in game. Bid 2NT to show your minimum hand with no support for either of his suits, but the diamonds stopped.

12) ♠ 6 4
    ♡ K 7 3
    ◇ A 3 2
    ♣ A J 10 6 4

West	East
1♡	2♣
2NT	?

Three hearts. Partner has 15 or 16 points so you want to play in game. He is also balanced, but he could still have a five-card suit in which case four hearts will be safer than 3NT. Three hearts tells him that you want to play in game but you have three hearts and are giving him a choice between four hearts and 3NT. He knows you do not have four hearts, as you would then have supported him immediately.

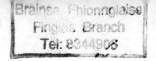

13) ♠ K J 4 3 2
    ♡ A 7
    ◇ A 10 4 2
    ♣ 9 7

West	East
1♡	1♠
2♣	?

Four spades. You have found a satisfactory trump suit and even opposite
a minimum opening bid you should have enough for game.

14) ♠ Q 10 8
    ♡ 6 4 2
    ◇ K J 8 7 3
    ♣ 7 4

West	East
1♣	1◇
1♠	?

Pass. If partner had wanted to compel you to bid again he could have
jumped. As he did not do so it is hard to see game being on with your bare
six points. You prefer spades so pass.

15) ♠ K J 4
    ♡ 7 2
    ◇ K Q 4
    ♣ A J 7 3 2

West	East
1♡	2♣
3♣	?

3NT. You have found a trump fit but five clubs is a long way to go with
such a balanced hand and nine tricks in no-trumps may prove easier than
eleven in clubs. Partner can always go back to clubs if he has a very shapely
hand and does not fancy no-trumps.

16) ♠ 7 3
    ♡ Q 3
    ◇ Q 10 8 2
    ♣ A J 10 6 4

West	East
1♡	2♣
3♡	?

Four hearts. Partner's jump rebid shows a good six-card suit and 16 plus
points so is forcing opposite your two-level response. ♡Q3 is quite adequate
support when partner is known to have a six-card suit.

17)	♠ K 10 7 3		**West**	**East**
	♡ 7		1♡	1♠
	◇ Q 10 8 6 4		3♡	?
	♣ J 7 3			

Pass. After a one-level response a jump rebid does not force you to bid again, and with an ill-fitting minimum you are best to pass. There is no question of bidding just because you dislike hearts, as there is no reason to suppose that anywhere else will be any better — not when partner has shown a good six-card suit.

18)	♠ Q 10 9 4		**West**	**East**
	♡ K J 6		1◇	1♠
	◇ K 10		1NT	?
	♣ 10 8 7 4			

2NT. Partner has a balanced 15–16 HCPs. You are happy in no-trumps but are unsure whether or not game is on. The raise to 2NT asks partner to bid game with a maximum but pass with a minimum.

19)	♠ Q 8 6		**West**	**East**
	♡ J 7 3 2		1♡	2♡
	◇ K 9 3		2NT	?
	♣ Q J 2			

3NT. Why is partner bidding no-trumps when you have agreed hearts? He must be inviting game or he would have just left two hearts, and he is trying to tell you that he has a balanced hand to help you to decide whether or not to bid the game. You are maximum so must accept the invitation, and as you are also balanced you should bid the game in no-trumps. Partner already knows that you have four hearts, so he can always go back to four hearts, if he so wishes.

20)	♠ Q 7 3 2		**West**	**East**
	♡ 8 6		1♣	1◇
	◇ K J 7 3 2		2♠	?
	♣ 10 4			

Three spades. Despite your minimum hand you must bid again when partner jumps in a new suit. Clearly you must raise spades with four-card support, and a simple raise to three will tell partner that you are weak.

Special Opening Bids
One No-Trump

The 1NT opening is a very precise bid. It promises 12–14 HCPs and a balanced hand, the definition of balanced being 4-3-3-3, 4-4-3-2 or 5-3-3-2 shape. It does not matter if you have a suit with no high card in it, but if you have a five-card suit it should not be a strong one, e.g. Q9863 is OK but AKJ107 is not — with a strong five-carder prefer to bid and rebid it.

Because 1NT is such a precise bid, partner is much more likely to be in a position to decide immediately on the final contract, than when facing a wide-ranging suit opening bid. Accordingly, the whole structure of bidding is different and the rules you have so painstakingly learned are of no use here, instead there is a new set.

Responding to 1NT

Responder has a balanced hand

0–10 points

Pass. There cannot be enough points for game and as you are both balanced 1NT should be as good as anywhere, e.g.

♠ 9 6 3
♡ Q 7 4 2
♢ K 8 3
♣ 7 6 4

11–12 points

Raise to 2NT. There may be the points for game, there may not. You are asking partner to pass with a minimum 1NT opener, but to bid 3NT with a maximum, for example:

♠ A 6 3
♡ Q 7 4 2
♢ K 8 3
♣ Q J 4

13–18 points

Raise to 3NT. When you have the points for game, bid it.

19–20 points

Raise to 4NT. This is one level higher than is necessary for game so is invitational to slam. Partner should pass with a minimum and bid 6NT with a maximum.

21 plus points

Raise straight to slam, 6NT

Responder has a long suit (five plus cards)

0–10 points

Bid two diamonds/two hearts/two spades. This is strictly to play and commands partner to pass. You are telling him that you think two of your suit will be a better contract than 1NT. Contrary to normal procedure, there is actually more case for making one of these bids the weaker your hand is. Say you hold:

♠ 10 8 7 6 4 2
♡ 9 5
◇ J 8
♣ 7 6 4

and partner opens 1NT. Your hand will probably be completely useless in no-trumps, but in spades, although you may have to lose to the missing top spades, you will eventually be the only person at the table with any trumps and will then be able to make tricks with them.

11 plus points

With a fairly balanced hand and a five-card minor suit, you are best to just raise no-trumps to the appropriate level. With a major, however, you should jump to three of your suit. This tells partner that you have at least a five-card suit and wish to play in game, so he must bid. You are asking him to choose between game in your suit and 3NT. He should not introduce a new suit. Bid three spades with:

52

♠ A J 10 7 4
♡ K 6
♢ A 6 4
♣ J 3 2

but 3NT with:

♠ J 3 2
♡ K 6
♢ A 6 4
♣ A J 10 7 4

With two five-card suits responder can jump in one and, if opener does not support it, try the other, for example: 1NT – 3♠ – 3NT – 4♡, to get partner to choose between the suits.

As responder has shown a five-card suit, opener need only have three to an honour, or three small plus a doubleton elsewhere, to support it.

Stayman

You may have noticed that 1NT – 2♢/2♡/2♠ were mentioned above, but not 1NT – 2♣. This is because two clubs is used in a special way over a 1NT opening. It asks opener if he has a four-card major suit, and is called **Stayman** after its inventor. You can only actually bid a suit in response to 1NT if you have at least five of them, yet a 4-4 fit will also give the necessary eight cards between the two hands to make a good trump suit. Four hearts or four spades on an eight-card fit will usually be a better contract than 3NT, and Stayman allows you to check back for such a fit. If you were intending to raise 1NT to 2NT or 3NT, and have one or more four-card majors, it costs you nothing to use Stayman on the way. If partner turns out not to have the suit you are looking for you can always go back to no-trumps on the next round.

The scheme looks like this:

1NT	2♣	
2♢		no 4-card major. It has nothing to do with diamonds, any more than the two club bid had to do with clubs.
2♡		four hearts
2♠		four spades

With both majors it is usual to bid hearts first, although it does not really matter very much so long as you are consistent.

53

1NT	2♣
2◇	2NT

11–12 points, invites 3NT just as an immediate 2NT would have done, for example:
- ♠ A J 7 4
- ♡ K 10 7 3
- ◇ K 6
- ♣ 10 9 7

3NT 13 plus points, to play, for example:
- ♠ A J 7 4
- ♡ K 10 7 3
- ◇ K 6
- ♣ Q 10 9

1NT	2♣
2♡	2NT

11–12 points, invites 3NT *but* opener may also bid spades if he has them because responder must have four. Why? He has bid two clubs so must have at least one major, yet he cannot have hearts or he would have supported them, for example he may have:
- ♠ A J 7 4
- ♡ K 6
- ◇ K 10 7 3
- ♣ 10 9 7

3NT 13 plus points. Opener may pass, but if he holds four spades he should bid four spades, as again responder must have spades for his two club bid.

3♡ 11–12 points, invites four hearts. Opener passes with a minimum but bids four hearts with a maximum.

4♡ 13 plus points, to play.

1NT	2♣
2♠	2NT
	3NT
	3♠
	4♠

2NT 11–12 points, invites 3NT
3NT 13 plus points, to play
3♠ 11–12 points, invites four spades
4♠ 13 plus points, to play

1NT	2♣
2 any	3♣

This cancels the first message and means that responder wishes he had never heard of Stayman and just wants to play in clubs — opener must now pass as three clubs shows a long suit but a weak hand, such as:

♠ K 6
♡ 7 3
♢ 10 4 2
♣ Q 9 8 7 6 3

As you will see if you work through the above scheme, it never costs to bid two clubs so long as you have at least one four-card major, as you can always bid no-trumps at your next turn if you wish, while you will often improve things if you find partner with the same suit as your own. Apart from the necessity of having at least one major yourself (otherwise what is the point of asking partner if he has one), the only other requirement is that you have sufficient strength to be able to cope with whatever partner's response may be. If you have, say:

♠ Q 4 3 2
♡ J 7 6 5
♢ 10 9 7 5 4
♣ —

you will be able to bid two clubs and pass any response, as if partner does not have a major you should have a reasonable number of diamonds between you. If, on the other hand, you do not have length in hearts, spades and diamonds, you are going to have to return to no-trumps if partner responds in a suit you are short in. To do that you will need at least 11 points because, as we have already seen, that is what two clubs followed by 2NT promises and is what partner will take you for.

QUIZ FIVE
The 1NT Opening

In each case, what is your next bid?

1) ♠ Q 8
   ♡ 987632
   ◇ 842
   ♣ J 3

West	East
1NT	?

2) ♠ A Q J 63
   ♡ K 62
   ◇ A 4
   ♣ 873

West	East
1NT	?

3) ♠ K 63
   ♡ K Q 4
   ◇ K 1092
   ♣ 1084

West	East
1NT	?

4) ♠ K 742
   ♡ A 6
   ◇ K J 9
   ♣ 10982

West	East
1NT	?

5) ♠ K 653
   ♡ Q 432
   ◇ 76
   ♣ K 93

West	East
1NT	?

6) ♠ A 73
   ♡ K J 4
   ◇ A J 73
   ♣ 1096

West	East
1NT	2♡
?	

7) ♠ Q J 42
   ♡ J 73
   ◇ A 7
   ♣ K J 93

West	East
1NT	2NT
?	

		West	East
8)	♠ 732	West	East
	♡ A K 4	1NT	2♣
	◇ Q 74	?	
	♣ A 10 8 3		

		West	East
9)	♠ Q 10 4	West	East
	♡ K 6	1NT	3♠
	◇ A 7 4 2	?	
	♣ K 10 8 4		

		West	East
10)	♠ K 7 4 2	West	East
	♡ A 6	1NT	2♣
	◇ K J 9	2♡	?
	♣ 10 9 8 2		

		West	East
11)	♠ Q 6 4 2	West	East
	♡ A K 7 3	1NT	2♣
	◇ K 10 7	2♡	3NT
	♣ J 4	?	

		West	East
12)	♠ K 6	West	East
	♡ A J 6 4	1NT	2♣
	◇ K 8 4 3	2♡	3♣
	♣ Q 7 2	?	

		West	East
13)	♠ A J 7 3	West	East
	♡ Q J 6	1NT	2♣
	◇ A Q 10 2	2♠	3♠
	♣ 7 3	?	

SOLUTIONS TO QUIZ FIVE
The 1NT Opening

1) ♠ Q8
   ♡ 987632
   ◇ 842
   ♣ J3

          West   East
          1NT   ?

Two hearts. This is a weak bid and tells partner to pass. It may seem strange to bid with such a poor hand, but just ask yourself "how many tricks will my hand make in no-trumps and how many with hearts as trumps?" You should then see that two hearts is likely to be a far better contract than 1NT.

2) ♠ AQJ63
   ♡ K62
   ◇ A4
   ♣ 873

          West   East
          1NT   ?

Three spades. With a long suit and a strong hand you must jump, as two spades would be to play. Three spades asks partner to bid four spades with three reasonable spades or 3NT with two, or three poor, spades.

3) ♠ K63
   ♡ KQ4
   ◇ K1092
   ♣ 1084

          West   East
          1NT   ?

2NT. With your balanced hand you are happy in no-trumps, so the only question is how high to go. If partner is maximum game should be on but not if he is minimum. 2NT invites game, leaving the final decision to partner.

4) ♠ K742
   ♡ A6
   ◇ KJ9
   ♣ 10982

          West   East
          1NT   ?

Two clubs. Again you have a raise to 2NT, but it cannot hurt to check for a 4-4 spade fit on the way. If partner responds two diamonds or two hearts you can now bid 2NT, but if he bids two spades you can raise to three spades.

5) ♠ K653   West   East
    ♡ Q432   1NT   ?
    ◇ 76
    ♣ K93

Pass. With a balanced hand but insufficient strength for game you must
pass. Two clubs may look superficially attractive as it will find a 4-4 major
suit fit if there is one, but the trouble comes when partner has to bid two
diamonds which leaves you with nowhere to go.

6) ♠ A73   West   East
    ♡ KJ4   1NT   2♡
    ◇ AJ73   ?
    ♣ 1096

Pass. It doesn't matter what your hand is, partner has told you to pass so
you must do so. He has a weak hand with a long heart suit.

7) ♠ QJ42   West   East
    ♡ J73   1NT   2NT
    ◇ A7   ?
    ♣ KJ93

Pass. Partner is inviting game and as you are minimum you must decline.

8) ♠ 732   West   East
    ♡ AK4   1NT   2♣
    ◇ Q74   ?
    ♣ A1083

Two diamonds. Partner's bid was Stayman, asking for a four-card major.
The response to show no major is two diamonds.

9) ♠ Q104   West   East
    ♡ K6   1NT   3♠
    ◇ A742   ?
    ♣ K1084

Four spades. Three spades is a strong bid showing at least five spades. With
Q104 you are quite happy to support partner's suit.

10) ♠ K742
    ♡ A6
    ◇ KJ9
    ♣ 10982

West	East
1NT	2♣
2♡	?

2NT. Still showing 11 or 12 points and inviting game just as if you had bid it directly over 1NT. If partner also has four spades, he will bid them. He knows you must have spades to have used two clubs, when you obviously do not have hearts.

11) ♠ Q642
    ♡ AK73
    ◇ K107
    ♣ J4

West	East
1NT	2♣
2♡	3NT
?	

Four spades. This is a tricky one, as you are already in game, but if you pause for a moment, you will see that partner must have four spades. He could not support hearts, yet he *must* have at least one four-card major to use Stayman.

12) ♠ K6
    ♡ AJ64
    ◇ K843
    ♣ Q72

West	East
1NT	2♣
2♡	3♣
?	

Pass. Partner wants to play in three clubs whatever your hand, he wasn't interested in the majors after all.

13) ♠ AJ73
    ♡ QJ6
    ◇ AQ102
    ♣ 73

West	East
1NT	2♣
2♠	3♠
?	

Four spades. Having found out about your four-card spade suit, partner is now inviting game. As you are maximum you accept the invitation.

Strong Openings

Opening bids at the two level show very strong hands, ones with which you would be afraid that if you opened with one of a suit and partner passed, you could have missed a game, even though that would mean that he had less than six points.

There are three different types of two opening which we have to consider.

(i) 2NT

This shows a balanced hand of about 20–22 HCPs. Because, like all no-trump bids, it gives a fairly precise picture of opener's hand straightaway, responder will often be in a good position to choose the final contract. The 2NT opening does not compel partner to bid, but he will obviously do so more often than not when facing what is known to be such a strong hand. The scheme of responses is as follows:

Pass

Any hand too weak to play in game, whatever the shape. There is no weakness take-out into a long suit of the type we saw over a 1NT opening. To go on to game responder needs roughly five points, four points and a five-card suit, or three points and a six-card suit, otherwise he passes.

3NT

To play. A flattish hand with 5–10 points, but could possibly have a long minor suit, as 3NT will often prove easier than five clubs/five diamonds, e.g.

♠ Q 6 3
♡ 7 4 2
◇ K J 6 5 2
♣ J 8

4NT

11–12 points in a balanced hand, and inviting slam in the same way as does 1NT – 4NT, for example:

61

♠ A 6 3
♡ K 4 2
◇ K J 6 5
♣ J 9 3

Three diamonds/three hearts/three spades

These are all natural bids, showing at least a five-card suit and the values for game or better, such as:

♠ A J 7 5 3
♡ K 6 2
◇ 9 4
♣ 7 3 2

Opener should choose between game in partner's suit and 3NT, in the same way as he does after 1NT – 3 of a suit.

Four hearts/four spades

At least a six-card suit and strictly to play, opener is not being asked to bid on. For example:

♠ Q 10 9 7 3 2
♡ K 6
◇ 8 4
♣ 7 3 2

If responder had been interested in slam he could have bid his suit at the three-level to see if opener liked the idea, e.g.:

♠ Q 9 8 7 3 2
♡ A K
◇ Q 4
♣ 7 3 2

Three clubs

This is Stayman (asking opener for a four-card major suit) and works in just the same way as when responding to 1NT. The scheme is:

2NT	3♣	
3◇		no four-card major, nothing to do with diamonds
3♡		four hearts, may or may not have four spades
3♠		four spades, denies four hearts

Remember that you should not bid three clubs unless you have at least one four-card major yourself — after all, what is the point?

(ii) Two diamonds/two hearts/two spades

These opening bids show very strong hands with at least a strong five-card suit. In deciding whether or not to open two of a suit, you do not so much count points as count likely playing tricks. For example, either AKQJx or AKJ9xx could be counted for five tricks assuming partner to hold two or three small in the suit. A two opening requires a hand of power and quality with at least eight sure, or nearly sure, playing tricks. A typical two heart opening might be:

♠ A 3
♡ A K Q 10 2
◇ K Q J 6 4
♣ 7

The reason for opening two rather than one is the fear that partner might pass a one opening and a good game contract be missed. After a two opening responder *must* bid, even with nothing, to give opener another chance. This will be particularly valuable if he has a second suit to show, as in the example above. The responses are as follows:

2NT

This is a negative. It is the bid with all bad hands irrespective of their shape and has nothing to do with a desire to play in no-trumps. It covers all hands of 0–6 points and also some stronger hands, which do not fit into any of the positive categories.

All other responses are positives.

Single raise, e.g. 2♡ - 3♡

This shows heart support and a hand which might have some potential for slam, usually, but not always, including at least one ace. Because opener has promised a long strong suit responder can support with as little as three small, queen doubleton, or better. For example:

♠ A 6
♡ 10 4 2
♢ K 7 4 3
♣ J 6 4 2

Double raise, e.g. 2♡ - 4♡

This shows heart support but denies an ace. This is the only real difference from the single raise as both show 7 plus points. The reason behind this is that with a positive response opposite a two opening, partner will often be thinking of a slam contract. Obviously, in a contract where you can only afford to lose one trick, aces are very important cards and the double raise warns partner off unless he has a lot of aces and kings himself, while a single raise would tend to encourage him to look beyond game. For example:

♠ K 6
♡ 10 4 2
♢ K 7 4 3
♣ Q J 4 2

3NT

A balanced hand with 10–12 HCPs but no genuine support for partner's suit.

A new suit

This promises at least seven points and a good five-card suit. Particularly with a minimum hand, it is important that most of your points be in the suit you bid. Since opener has promised a very good suit there is no point in offering an alternative unless it also is reasonable, such as 2♡ – 3♢ with:

♠ K J 3
♡ 8 6
♢ A Q 10 7 4
♣ 7 4 2

After a positive response the bidding must continue until at least the game level has been reached. Bidding is on normal lines, each player showing his suits until a satisfactory fit has been found.

After the negative 2NT response, opener must bid again — after all, responder has not said that he wants to play in no-trumps, merely that he has a
poor hand. Opener bids a second suit, rebids a very long first suit, or bids
3NT if fairly balanced. Unless opener jumps, responder is allowed to pass
if he has a really weak hand, but should bid game if he has a couple of
useful looking cards. When partner is known to have a shapely hand, aces
and kings are always likely to be useful, but lower honours may not be
unless in partner's suit, so simply counting points will not help, judgement
of what might be useful will be needed. For example, after 2♠ – 2NT –
3♠, responder should pass with:

> ♠ Q 7
> ♡ J 5 4 3 2
> ◇ J 6 3
> ♣ J 10 4

which has only one useful card — the queen of spades — but raise to four
spades with:

> ♠ Q 7
> ♡ 8 5 4 3 2
> ◇ K 6 3
> ♣ 10 4 2

In the latter case the king and queen are both likely to be worth a trick to
partner.

(iii) Two clubs

The two club opening is a completely artificial bid, in other words it has
nothing whatsoever to do with clubs. It shows 23 plus points or a game-going
hand and, with one exception, is forcing to game, even if responder has
nothing. It means that a player holding a very powerful hand but with no
clear idea what should be trumps can explore all the possibilities, without
having to keep jumping just to force partner to keep bidding. Two clubs is
a rare bid but a very important one, as the rewards for accurate bidding of
very big hands are so large. For example, open two clubs on:

> ♠ K Q 10 4
> ♡ A K 6 4 2
> ◇ A K
> ♣ A Q

Responding to two clubs

Two diamonds

This is a negative response and covers all hands with 0–6 points, and some 7 or 8 point hands that don't fit in anywhere else start by bidding two diamonds.

Two hearts/two spades

These responses show 7 plus points and a reasonable five-card, or good four-card, suit. Roughly, the minimum suit quality should be about QJxxx or KQxx.

2NT

This shows 7–9 HCPs and a flattish hand. It may include a five-card suit which is too weak to bid, such as:

$$♠ \; J7642$$
$$♡ \; K3$$
$$♢ \; Q64$$
$$♣ \; Q83$$

Three clubs/three diamonds

These responses show 7 plus points and a reasonable five-card suit. When you are going up a level like this you should have more than just a four-card suit.

3NT

This shows 10–12 HCPs and a balanced hand.

2♣ - 2♢ - 2NT

This shows a balanced hand with 23 or 24 points, the next range up over a 2NT opening bid. It is the only rebid which responder is allowed to pass, indeed any other rebid by opener commits his side to reach at least game. With nothing, responder passes, otherwise he bids in just the same way as if partner had opened 2NT, except that he allows for the fact that partner is stronger to bid two clubs first. In other words, his bids have the same meaning after 2♣ – 2◇ – 2NT as after a 2NT opening: three clubs is Stayman, three of another suit shows at least five and is forcing, and so on.

All other sequences are forcing to game, whether the first response was the two diamond negative or a positive. Bidding goes along normal lines with each player bidding his suits in turn, longest first, until a suitable contract is found, as in this example:

	♠ A K Q 7 4			♠ 10 6
	♡ A K J 3	N		♡ 10 9 4 2
	◇ A Q 2	W E		◇ 9 4
	♣ 10	S		♣ Q J 7 6 3

West	East
2♣	2◇
2♠	3♣
3♡	4♡

West opens two clubs with his 23 points; East responds two diamonds with his 3 HCPs; West bids his longest suit; East bids his longest suit; West rebids in a second four-card suit; East is happy to raise to four hearts with his four-card support and West is happy to pass.

QUIZ SIX
Two Openings

In each case, what is your next bid?

			West	East
1)	♠ 73 ♡ 1076532 ◇ 974 ♣ 62		2NT	?
2)	♠ QJ62 ♡ KJ74 ◇ 3 ♣ 8762		2NT	?
3)	♠ K10 ♡ Q62 ◇ AK104 ♣ AKJ2		2NT ?	3♡
4)	♠ AKQ ♡ QJ3 ◇ KJ ♣ AJ632		2NT ?	3♣
5)	♠ AKQ ♡ K1064 ◇ J63 ♣ AKJ		2NT ?	4♡
6)	♠ 6543 ♡ K73 ◇ A642 ♣ Q3		2♡	?
7)	♠ J4 ♡ AKJ103 ◇ 876 ♣ J42		2♠	?

8)   ♠ J107642   **West**   **East**
      ♡ K3   2◇   ?
      ◇ 76
      ♣ 942

9)   ♠ AKJ1097   **West**   **East**
      ♡ AK3   2♠   2NT
      ◇ KJ2   ?
      ♣ 7

10)   ♠ AKJ109   **West**   **East**
      ♡ AQJ4   2♠   2NT
      ◇ AK   ?
      ♣ 72

11)   ♠ 732   **West**   **East**
      ♡ Q1042   2♠   2NT
      ◇ 863   3◇   ?
      ♣ J42

12)   ♠ Q7   **West**   **East**
      ♡ K632   2♠   2NT
      ◇ 764   3♣   ?
      ♣ J732

13)   ♠ 104   **West**   **East**
      ♡ 8632   2♣   ?
      ◇ A93
      ♣ J432

14)   ♠ 732   **West**   **East**
      ♡ A4   2♣   ?
      ◇ KQ1042
      ♣ 1094

15)   ♠ Q73   **West**   **East**
      ♡ KJ64   2♣   ?
      ◇ 1093
      ♣ QJ2

16) ♠ Q72
♡ J43
♢ 72
♣ 108643

West	East
2♣	2♢
2NT	?

17) ♠ J6
♡ J4
♢ Q10732
♣ 10743

West	East
2♣	2♢
2♡	?

18) ♠ KQ6
♡ AKJ4
♢ A
♣ AQJ104

West	East
2♣	2♢
3♣	3♢
?	

SOLUTIONS TO QUIZ SIX
Two Openings

1) ♠ 73
    ♡ 1076532
    ◇ 974
    ♣ 62

    West   East
    2NT   ?

Pass. With a long suit and a weak hand you would like to be able to play in three hearts, unfortunately there is no way that you can do so, as partner will bid again if you do bid three hearts, expecting you to have a better hand. Weak hands must pass a 2NT opening and just hope that partner can manage eight tricks.

2) ♠ QJ62
    ♡ KJ74
    ◇ 3
    ♣ 8762

    West   East
    2NT   ?

Three clubs. You have the points for game, and could just raise to 3NT. If partner also has four cards in a major, however, game in that suit will probably be safer, so it is best to check via a Stayman three club bid. You can always bid 3NT on the next round if he denies a major.

3) ♠ K10
    ♡ Q62
    ◇ AK104
    ♣ AKJ2

    West   East
    2NT   3♡
    ?

Four hearts. Partner has shown five hearts and the strength to play in game. ♡Q62 is ample support, so you should raise him.

4) ♠ AKQ
    ♡ QJ3
    ◇ KJ
    ♣ AJ632

    West   East
    2NT   3♣
    ?

Three diamonds. Partner's three clubs was Stayman, asking for a four-card major suit. Three diamonds does not show diamonds, it merely denies a major.

5)	♠ A K Q		West	East
	♡ K 10 6 4		2NT	4♡
	◇ J 6 3		?	
	♣ A K J			

Pass. Partner has selected the contract and expects you to pass whatever your hand.

6)	♠ 7 5 4 3		West	East
	♡ K 7 3		2♡	?
I	◇ A 6 4 2			
	♣ Q 3			

Three hearts. ♡K73 is ample support for a two opening. Three hearts promises positive values (seven plus points) and heart support, usually though not always with at least one ace — exactly what you have.

7)	♠ J 4		West	East
	♡ A K J 10 3		2♠	?
	◇ 8 7 6			
	♣ J 4 2			

Three hearts. This shows a good five-card heart suit and positive values and is, of course, forcing to game.

8)	♠ J 10 7 6 4 2		West	East
	♡ K 3		2◇	?
J	◇ 7 6			
	♣ 9 4 2			

2NT. You may be able to show your spades on the next round, but to bid two spades now would promise a better hand than this. 2NT is the negative response on *all* weak hands.

9)	♠ A K J 10 9 7		West	East
	♡ A K 3		2♠	2NT
	◇ K J 2		?	
	♣ 7			

Three spades. You must bid again, and clearly the only thing you can do is to rebid the excellent spade suit. Three spades is sufficient, as you have no reason to think that you can make ten tricks unless partner has some help for you, in which case he can bid the game.

10)   ♠ A K J 10 9

     ♡ A Q J 4

     ♢ A K

     ♣ 7 2

West	East
2♠	2NT
?	

Three hearts. This is better than three spades because it gives partner some new information — he already knows you have five spades — and offers him a choice of suits.

11)   ♠ 7 3 2

     ♡ Q 10 4 2

     ♢ 8 6 3

     ♣ J 4 2

West	East
2♠	2NT
3♢	?

Three spades. You are too weak to do other than choose between partner's suits as cheaply as possible. As usual, with no real preference you return to his first suit, as it may prove to be longer than the second.

12)   ♠ Q 7

     ♡ K 6 3 2

     ♢ 7 6 4

     ♣ J 7 3 2

West	East
2♠	2NT
3♠	?

Four spades. ♠Q7 is good support when partner has opened two then rebid his suit as he must have at least six. You have two good cards — the queen of spades and king of hearts — so there is a good chance of game being on.

13)   ♠ 10 4

     ♡ 8 6 3 2

     ♢ A 9 3

     ♣ J 4 3 2

West	East
2♣	?

Two diamonds. This has nothing to do with diamonds, but is the first response on all bad hands.

14)   ♠ 7 3 2

     ♡ A 4

     ♢ K Q 10 4 2

     ♣ 10 9 4

West	East
2♣	?

Three diamonds. This time you have enough for a positive response, nine points and a good five-card suit. Two diamonds would be a negative so you must jump to three diamonds to show your good hand.

73

15)	♠ Q73	West	East
	♡ KJ64	2♣	?
	◇ 1093		
	♣ QJ2		

2NT. 7–9 HCPs and a balanced hand. With your high cards nicely scattered, what could describe your hand better?

16)	♠ Q72	West	East
	♡ J43	2♣	2◇
	◇ 72	2NT	?
	♣ 108643		

3NT. Only three points, but partner has shown 23 or 24, so while 3NT may not always be a success it should pay to bid it in the long run.

17)	♠ J6	West	East
	♡ J4	2♣	2◇
	◇ Q10732	2♡	?
	♣ 10743		

Three diamonds. You are not keen on partner's hearts, so as you must bid something, try your longest suit. Remember that you have not yet bid diamonds, as your initial bid was just showing a weak hand.

18)	♠ KQ6	West	East
	♡ AKJ4	2♣	2◇
	◇ A	3♣	3◇
	♣ AQJ104	?	

Three hearts. So, partner has a weak hand with a diamond suit and does not like clubs. There is no reason why he cannot have four hearts, so continue to bid out the shape of your hand, rather than a lazy 3NT.

Pre-emptive Opening Bids

Opening bids at the three level and higher are known as pre-emptive openings. They are all based on a very long suit but a fairly low point count — usually less than would be required to open at the one level. The idea behind these bids is that, with relatively few high cards, the hand probably belongs to your opponents and, by opening at a high level, you make it very difficult for them to get together and find their best contract. The fact that you have such a long suit means that even if partner turns up with nothing, you should not get into too much trouble, and even going down a couple of tricks may be a good investment, if the opposition could have made something their way if left to themselves.

Three of a suit

This shows a reasonable seven-card suit and up to about 10 HCPs. Ideally, most of the strength should be in the long suit. The exact strength varies a little depending on the vulnerability — obviously going down costs more vulnerable than not. The traditional requirement has been that you have roughly six playing tricks non-vulnerable and seven vulnerable, so that even if you are doubled you can only lose 500 points. That is a good basis to work on, but you can certainly afford to loosen up a little, so long as the main suit is a good one, as opponents tend to be loth to double unless they have good trumps themselves. Certainly it would be a bit wet not to open three with KJ10xxxx non-vulnerable or KQJ10xxx vulnerable, even with nothing outside, though both are theoretically a trick short.

The other traditional rule has been that you should not pre-empt if you have a four-card major on the side, in case you talk your own side out of a fit in that major. At risk of being accused of blasphemy, I would say that pre-emption makes life so difficult for your opponents that even this rule can be partially ignored. I would open three with a weak four-card major on the side. With a strong four-card side suit (major or minor), I would not consider a three-level opening.

♠ 7 6 3 2
♡ K J 10 8 7 6 4
♢ 7
♣ 3

would be a three heart opening, but:

♠ A J 10 2
♡ Q J 9 7 6 3 2
♢ 8
♣ 4

would not.

Responding to a three opening

The opening bid is very precise, a good seven-card suit but little else, probably useless with any other suit as trumps. This means that responder is in an excellent position to pick the final contract. Far more often than not he will choose to pass. Even many hands which would have been worth an opening bid in their own right should pass when partner opens at the three-level, e.g.

♠ Q J 6
♡ Q J 6
♢ A 8 4
♣ Q J 6 3

When responder does bid, his choice will usually be between raising to game in opener's suit and bidding 3NT; a new suit bid is very rare.

As usual, when partner is known to have a shapely hand, merely counting points will not be sufficient to decide whether or not to raise to game. Responder should instead count tricks — aces are always tricks, kings often are, queens and jacks rarely, as they tend to come into their own too late, when declarer only has one or two cards in the suit. If he thinks that he can see where ten tricks will come from, he may raise to game. Even then he has to consider whether there may be four losers before the ten winners can be set up. For example, a suit of QJ109 will produce two winners eventually, but probably far too late — Axxx, one sure trick, is likely to be a better holding. Raise three spades to four spades (vulnerable) with:

♠ J 7
♡ A 7 6 3
♢ A 8 6 4
♣ A 7 6

but pass with:

♠ J 7
♡ Q J 10 9
♢ A 8 6 4
♣ A 7 6

When considering bidding 3NT, responder only needs to be able to count nine tricks, but again he has to consider the possibility of losing five tricks, before the nine winners can be cashed. Usually, having one wide open suit is sufficient to make 3NT a bad risk. The other important consideration is that opener's suit is likely to be needed as a primary source of tricks. That means that declarer is going to have to have a way of getting to opener's hand to cash those tricks. A shortage in opener's suit can be a serious handicap to this, and we find ourselves in a strange situation where responder may bid 3NT with a good fit in opener's suit yet raise the suit with only a small singleton in support on another hand.

If responder does bid a new suit he should have a powerful hand with a very good suit, e.g. bid three hearts over three clubs with:

♠ A K 7
♡ A Q J 9 6 4
♢ 8 3
♣ K 7

Remember, if you find opener with three small cards in your suit you will have been very fortunate. Opener must bid again and should support partner's suit with three small or a doubleton honour, otherwise he will usually rebid his own suit.

So far we have assumed that responder is only bidding on because he expects to make game; there is, however, a second reason why he might raise opener's suit. Say partner opens three hearts and you hold:

♠ 7
♡ Q 6 4 2
♢ 7 3 2
♣ J 9 5 3 2

You know that you have eleven hearts between you and virtually no other high cards, so the opposition must have a big fit elsewhere and can surely make a slam. Partner has made life awkward for them by opening at the three level, you can make it even harder by raising to four hearts or five hearts. You don't expect to make your contract, but maybe they will settle for doubling you or even bid the wrong slam if you put them under enough pressure. Small minuses are very good scores when your opponents could be getting a big plus score instead.

The 3NT opening

This is a rare opening bid and is used to show a completely solid seven- or eight-card minor suit and little or nothing else. If responder thinks there is a chance of running nine tricks he passes, otherwise he can bid four clubs or five clubs, and opener will pass or convert to diamonds, if that is his suit.

Four of a suit

This opening is just a bigger version of the three opening, showing a seven- or eight-card suit and fairly low point count. Something around eight playing tricks are required, and while the point count can go into double figures, it should not get near to that associated with a strong two opening. Though the playing strength may be similar, the defensive potential is much lower, e.g.:

♠ A Q J 10 8 7 6 3
♡ 7
◇ 5
♣ Q J 9

QUIZ SEVEN
Pre-emptive Openings

You are not vulnerable. What is your bid?

		West	East
1)	♠ KQ108732 ♡ 73 ◇ J4 ♣ 62	?	
2)	♠ 7 ♡ 10865432 ◇ A2 ♣ 763	?	
3)	♠ J ♡ AQJ109832 ◇ K2 ♣ 76	?	
4)	♠ 9 ♡ AJ108732 ◇ 7 ♣ AQ64	?	
5)	♠ KJ32 ♡ 762 ◇ KQ6 ♣ QJ10	3♡	?
6)	♠ AK74 ♡ 6 ◇ AK53 ♣ AJ62	3♡	?
7)	♠ A10732 ♡ A6 ◇ AQJ ♣ J42	3♡	?

8) ♠ QJ4
♥ AJ3
♦ A1072
♣ A63

West	East
3♥	?

9) ♠ 64
♥ KJ109732
♦ K2
♣ 83

West	East
3♥	3NT
?	

10) ♠ 9
♥ AJ108732
♦ Q5
♣ 762

West	East
3♥	4♣
?	

SOLUTIONS TO QUIZ SEVEN
Pre-emptive Openings

1)   ♠ K Q 10 8 7 3 2   **West**   **East**
      ♡ 7 3   ?
      ◇ J 4
      ♣ 6 2

Three spades. A perfect textbook example of a non-vulnerable three opening. When responding to a three opening, try assuming partner has roughly this hand. Now look at your own hand and see whether the contract you are thinking of bidding would be likely to succeed. If the answer is yes, bid it, otherwise look for an alternative.

2)   ♠ 7   **West**   **East**
      ♡ 10 8 6 5 4 3 2   ?
      ◇ A 2
      ♣ 7 6 3

Pass. Your hearts are far too weak, increasing the danger of being doubled and, even with the ace outside, you are nowhere near to the six tricks you are promising if you open three hearts.

3)   ♠ J   **West**   **East**
      ♡ A Q J 10 9 8 3 2   ?
      ◇ K 2
      ♣ 7 6

Four hearts. This time you are just too good to open only three hearts. After all, you would do that if the ace of hearts were turned into a small spade — a hand which would be two tricks worse than your actual one. The low point count does suggest a preempt, however, and four hearts will be much tougher for your opponents to handle than a one heart opening would be.

4) ♠ 9   West   East
    ♡ A J 10 8 7 3 2   ?
    ◇ 7
    ♣ A Q 6 4

One heart. You are far too good for three hearts, and, while some would therefore open four, the good club suit makes this risky as a good contract could be missed in that suit.

5) ♠ K J 3 2   West   East
    ♡ 7 6 2   3♡   ?
    ◇ K Q 6
    ♣ Q J 10

Pass. Twelve points do not make game. It is much easier to see four or more losers than it is to see 10 tricks.

6) ♠ A K 7 4   West   East
    ♡ 6   3♡   ?
    ◇ A K 5 3
    ♣ A J 6 2

Four hearts. With five quick tricks it must be worth a shot at game. The instinctive reaction is to bid 3NT because you do not like hearts, but that is precisely why you should not bid no-trumps. In four hearts it is easy to get to partner's hand by ruffing; in 3NT you may never get there — and do you fancy trying to make nine tricks all out of your own hand?

7) ♠ A 10 7 3 2   West   East
    ♡ A 6   3♡   ?
    ◇ A Q J
    ♣ J 4 2

Four hearts. Game is by no means certain, possibly requiring a successful diamond finesse, for example, but it must have a good chance. There is no point bidding the spades, as your combined heart holding must be better and the weakness in clubs rules out no-trumps.

8)   ♠ QJ4
     ♡ AJ3
     ◇ A 10 7 2
     ♣ A 6 3

West	East
3♡	?

3NT. Despite the heart fit, 3NT is better than four hearts. Count the tricks and you will see that with any luck there are seven hearts plus two aces, making nine, so with every suit covered, 3NT should be OK, but the tenth trick in four hearts may be one too many.

9)   ♠ 64
     ♡ K J 10 9 7 3 2
     ◇ K 2
     ♣ 83

West	East
3♡	3NT
?	

Pass. Partner knows what to expect for your three-level opening and has picked the final contract. You should trust him and pass automatically.

10) ♠ 9
     ♡ A J 10 8 7 3 2
     ◇ Q 5
     ♣ 762

West	East
3♡	4♣
?	

Five clubs. It must be right to support partner, as he could hardly hope for better club support than this after your three heart opening.

SECTION TWO
THE CONTESTED AUCTION

The opponents open with one of a suit

The overcall

When an opponent has opened the bidding in front of you, you are in a very different situation from when you are the first to speak, consequently the rules which you have so painstakingly learnt have to be in some cases modified and in others thrown out completely. Partly this is because it has become a little more dangerous to bid now that one opponent already knows that his partner has a good hand. The other reason is that some bids have been taken away from you; if someone has opened one heart, for example, you can no longer bid one club, one diamond or one heart yourself. A new scheme is called for to overcome these problems.

If you bid a new suit over an opponent's opening bid you are making what is known as an **overcall**. At the one level an overcall promises a reasonable five-card or longer suit and around 8–15 points, while, as usual, a little more is needed to bid at the two-level, roughly 11–15 points. The major change to remember is that while you may open the bidding with a four-card suit, to overcall you must have at least five. This is largely for reasons of safety; if you bid a ropey four-card suit and the next player holds length in the same suit, he may double you and score a large penalty. Over one heart the following would be reasonable one spade and two diamond overcalls respectively:

♠ K J 9 7 6　　　　　　♠ K 3
♡ 8 7 3　　　　　　　　♡ 8 7 3
◇ A 6　　　　　　　　　◇ A Q 10 9 6
♣ 10 4 2　　　　　　　♣ K 4 2

Responding to an overcall

When partner overcalls you may respond with as few as six points if you have support for his suit, and because he is known to have at least five you only need to have three trumps to raise him. A single raise would show up to about ten points, a jump raise (1♡ - 3♡) about 11–13, and a raise to game at least 14.

If you do not have support for partner you should pass with less than about nine or ten points, even if you dislike his suit quite strongly, e.g. pass a one heart overcall with:

♠ A 9 7 4
♡ 6
♢ K Q 10 9
♣ 6 4 3 2

but should try to find a bid once you get up to about ten points or more. The reason why you can pass with 6–9 points (hands which would respond to an opening bid) is that when partner overcalls he is limited to around 15 points. If you have less than ten points, it is unlikely that there will be a game on unless you have a fit for his suit.

If you are not supporting partner, you may bid either no-trumps or a new suit. If no-trumps, you must as always make a limit bid, in other words the stronger your hand the more you bid. Roughly, 1NT shows 9–11 HCPs, 2NT 12–14 and 3NT 15 plus, in response to a one-level overcall. If the overcall was at the two-level, you would bid 2NT on around 10–12 HCPs and 3NT with 13 plus — you need less because partner has promised more. There is one other very important requirement for a bid of no-trumps, and that is that you must have at least one sure stopper in the opponent's suit. In other words, if they lead their suit, as is very likely, you will get in at least once before they can run it all against you.

A new suit response to an overcall should almost always be at least a five-card suit, and while not forcing partner to speak again is highly encouraging, so he should go on if he has a good hand for his overcall. If you do want to make the overcaller bid again you can always jump in your suit to show a very good hand.

The jump overcall

A jump overcall, e.g. one heart on your right, two spades from you, shows 12–16 points and a six-card suit (occasionally a very strong five-card suit). Partner will assume that a doubleton is sufficient support as you have promised such a long strong suit by your jump. Again, for partner to bid no-trumps would require a stopper in the opponents' suit. Indeed, this is a blanket rule to cover all situations where the opponents have bid: the first member of your side to bid no-trumps *must* have their suit covered. After all, what do you think they are going to lead?

The 1NT overcall

With a balanced hand and at least one sure stopper in the opener's suit you can overcall in no-trumps. Although a 1NT opening can be made on as little as 12–14 HCPs, it would be very dangerous to *overcall* on such a weak hand, as the third player is ideally placed to double you whenever he has upwards of eight or nine points and knows that his side has the balance of strength. With no long suit to escape into, you could concede a sizeable penalty. To make this less likely, experience has shown that 15–17 HCPs is a better range for a 1NT overcall, as you are less likely to get doubled, and even if you are, you have extra strength so the penalty should not be too large, e.g. bid 1◇ – 1NT on:

♠ A 7 3
♡ Q 6 4
◇ A J 10 3
♣ K Q 6

It is best to respond to a 1NT overcall in exactly the same way as to a 1NT opening. In other words, if partner overcalls 1NT, two clubs is Stayman, two of a suit is to play, and three of a suit is strong and forcing. The only adjustment needed is to allow for the fact that a 1NT overcaller is stronger than a 1NT opener, so responder needs correspondingly less to be interested in game.

The take-out double

You will have noticed that to overcall in a suit you need at least five cards, and that even strong balanced hands cannot overcall no-trumps unless they include a stopper in the opponents' suit. What do you do when you have the points to want to bid but there is nothing you can overcall? The answer is to *double*. Where a double is the first positive bid made by your side, it is for take-out, asking partner to tell you firstly his longest suit, other than that bid by the opposition, and secondly his strength.

An ideal doubling hand is one with four cards in all the unbid suits and therefore short in opener's suit. With this perfect shape you need about 11–12 HCPs upwards to double. As the shape gets away from the ideal, you may still double but must have extra high-card strength to compensate. So with a singleton in opener's suit you may double with 12 plus HCPs, with a doubleton you need 14 plus, while if you have three cards in it 15 plus HCPs are required.

Double a one club opening bid with any of the following hands:

♠ A 7 6 3	♠ A J 6 3	♠ A J 6 3
♡ K J 8 4	♡ A J 8 4	♡ A Q 8
◇ K J 9 7	◇ K J 7	◇ K J 7
♣ 5	♣ 8 2	♣ 10 7 3

The essential difference is that you overcall when you have a distinct preference for one suit over the others and wish to *tell* partner about it, while you double when you want to bid but do not have a clear preference, and so need to *ask* partner to choose a suit.

Responding to the take-out double

If the third player passes, you must respond to a take-out double even with nothing. That may sound risky, but in reality the alternative of passing with a weak hand is far more dangerous, as they will almost certainly make their doubled contract, probably with overtricks. Remember that partner is likely to be short in their suit, so if you have a weak hand where are the tricks to come from to beat the contract? Usually, you will respond by bidding your longest suit, the scheme being as follows, for example:

1♡ - Double - Pass - ?

| 1♠/2♣/2◇ | 0–8 points and is your longest suit. With two suits of equal length you follow the same rules as for opening, i.e. bid the cheaper of four-card suits, the higher of five-card suits, e.g. bid one spade with: |

      ♠ Q764
      ♡ 963
      ◇ 8742
      ♣ Q3

| 2♠/3♣/3◇ | 9–12 points and is your longest suit, e.g. bid two spades with: |

      ♠ A764
      ♡ 963
      ◇ A742
      ♣ Q3

| 1NT | 6–10 points and promises a good stopper in the opponent's suit and a balanced hand e.g.: |

      ♠ J63
      ♡ Q1074
      ◇ A97
      ♣ J104

2NT   11–12 points, a good stopper, and a balanced hand, e.g.:

                            ♠ K63
                            ♡ KJ74
                            ♢ A97
                            ♣ J104

Pass   Very rare, but it shows very strong trumps, almost certainly better than opener's — something like KQJ10x or QJ109x. You are not passing out of weakness, but out of a positive desire to defend against their contract and hopefully collect a useful penalty.

With 13 or more points, slightly less with a long suit, you should want to play in game as there must be at least 25 points between the two hands. With a double stopper you can bid 3NT, while with a long suit you can jump to game in the suit. There will be some hands with which you will have the strength for game but will be unsure which game will prove best. In that case you need to ask partner's opinion, and the way to do this is to bid the opponents' suit, e.g. 1♡ - Double - Pass - 2♡. This may look odd, but it is the one suit you could never want to bid in an attempt to play there. After all, if you thought you could make two hearts, wouldn't you just pass and leave them to stew in one heart doubled? Two hearts making scores +110; one heart doubled minus two scores +300 or +500 according to vulnerability — far more lucrative. As you could not want to play in two hearts, that bid is available for a special meaning — "Partner, I want to play in game but don't know which one. Please keep bidding your suits (longest first) until we find one which suits us both" — and has nothing at all to do with the suit you actually bid. This idea may take a little getting used to, but it can be very useful, and is not really any stranger than, for example, bidding two clubs as Stayman rather than to actually show a club suit, e.g. bid two hearts on:

                     ♠ A942
                     ♡ 7
                     ♢ KQ73
                     ♣ KJ98

I have said that responder to the double must bid something if the third player passes. If that player bids, however, he relieves you of that obligation. This is for two reasons: firstly, the double has now been taken out and there is no longer the danger of them making a doubled contract plus overtricks, and, secondly, partner will get a second chance, in case he has a very big hand, whether you bid or not. Responder should still bid if he has anything useful to show, but may pass if very weak. After 1♡ - Double - 1♠, bid two clubs with:

♠ Q 9 3
♡ 7 4 2
♢ 8 7
♣ A 10 9 6 3

but pass with:

♠ Q 9 3
♡ 7 4 2
♢ 8 7
♣ 10 9 6 3 2

Even opposite a passed partner, the doubler may bid again with a very good hand. In these two situations:

1♡	Dble	2♡	Pass		1♡	Dble	2♣	Pass
Pass	Dble				2♡	Dble		

the second double is again for take-out, merely showing a better hand. e.g.:

♠ A Q 7 4
♡ 8
♢ A K 9 4
♣ K J 10 5

After all, you could hardly want to make a take-out double of one heart, then suddenly want to make a penalty double of two hearts, when partner has shown nothing, could you? That would be a strange hand indeed.

The doubler rebids, e.g. 1♡ - Double - Pass - anything - Pass - ?

Unless there is a chance of game, the doubler should normally pass on the next round. He has asked partner to pick a suit and should abide by his decision. This is why it is so important that partner not only shows his suit but also the strength of his hand when responding to the double. If he did not do so, you would be completely in the dark and would always have to bid again, in case he had a good hand and game was on. As it is, however, you can be confident that if he makes a simple response in a suit he is limited to at most eight points, so you will need at least 17 or more to consider bidding again. Even when partner jumps in a suit, showing a reasonable hand, you know that he was unable to bid game himself, so unless you have something to spare for your double, you can still pass.

If the doubler does decide to bid again, he will usually be supporting responder's suit. As always, the more he bids the stronger his hand. For example:

1♡	Dble	Pass	1♠
Pass	2♠		

2♠ I know you have only 0–8 points but game could still be on if you are right at the top end of that range, say seven or eight points. Please bid on if you have a maximum, otherwise pass.

3♠ A strong invitation to game. If I needed you to be maximum for game to be on I would have only bid two spades, so this means I am so strong that I think game should be on unless you are minimum. Even an average four or five points could be enough, so please bid game if you have anything which looks useful and only pass with a complete bust.

Having asked partner to pick the suit, if the doubler overrules him by bidding another suit, e.g. 1♡ – Double – Pass – 1♠ – Pass – 2◇, he is showing a five-card suit in a strong hand, one which was too good to merely overcall on initially, e.g.

♠ A Q 3
♡ 9 2
◇ A K J 10 9
♣ A 7 2

He is showing, therefore, around 16 points upwards and responder should strain to keep the bidding open if he has anything, as the doubler may need very little help for game to be on. If the doubler wants to force responder to bid a second time, he can always jump in a new suit at his second turn, thereby showing a very powerful hand indeed.

QUIZ EIGHT

The opponents open one of a suit

Your right-hand opponent opens one diamond. What do you bid?

1) ♠ A Q 10 7 3
   ♡ K 9
   ◇ 7 6 4 2
   ♣ J 3

2) ♠ 7 3 2
   ♡ Q 4
   ◇ A 6
   ♣ A Q 10 8 7 3

3) ♠ A J 4
   ♡ Q 6 2
   ◇ A J 4
   ♣ K J 10 7

4) ♠ A Q 4
   ♡ K 6 2
   ◇ 1 0 7 4
   ♣ A K 10 7

5) ♠ A K J 6 3 2
   ♡ A K Q
   ◇ 7 3
   ♣ 9 4

6) ♠ A Q J 4
   ♡ K 10 9 3
   ◇ 6
   ♣ A 8 7 2

What is your next bid?

7) ♠ K 7 2
   ♡ 6 3
   ◇ A 10 4 3 2
   ♣ Q 6 2

West	North	East	South
1♡	1♠	Pass	?

8) ♠ 7 2
   ♡ J 5 4
   ◇ A K 10 8 6 3
   ♣ A 2

West	North	East	South
1♡	1♠	Pass	?

9) ♠ J 10 4
   ♡ 6 3
   ◇ A 8 3 2
   ♣ K 6 4 2

West	North	East	South
1♡	2♣	Pass	?

10) ♠ 10 9 8 3
    ♡ K J 10
    ◇ K J 4
    ♣ K 6 4

West	North	East	South
1♡	2♣	Pass	?

11) ♠ Q 6 3
    ♡ 7
    ◇ A 8 6 4 2
    ♣ J 10 7 2

West	North	East	South
1♡	2♠	Pass	?

91

		West	North	East	South
12)	♠ 976532 ♡ J4 ◇ 862 ♣ J3	1♡	1NT	Pass	?
13)	♠ 10643 ♡ J103 ◇ 764 ♣ Q83	1◇	Dble	Pass	?
14)	♠ J83 ♡ 10643 ◇ 7632 ♣ 94	1◇	Dble	1♠	?
15)	♠ K7 ♡ A863 ◇ 9432 ♣ QJ4	1◇	Dble	Pass	?
16)	♠ AJ64 ♡ AJ64 ◇ A2 ♣ 1093	1◇	Dble	Pass	?
17)	♠ K1096 ♡ AJ43 ◇ 72 ♣ AK3	1◇ Pass	Dble ?	Pass	1♡
18)	♠ KQ105 ♡ KQ7 ◇ 7 ♣ K10983	1◇ Pass	Dble ?	Pass	2◇
19)	♠ AK72 ♡ AK72 ◇ 103 ♣ A94	1◇ Pass	Dble ?	Pass	1♡

SOLUTIONS TO QUIZ EIGHT

The opponents open one of a suit

1) ♠ A Q 10 7 3
   ♡ K 9
   ◇ 7 6 4 2
   ♣ J 3

West	North	East	South
1◇	?		

One spade. Ten points and a good five-card suit, ample for a simple overcall at the one level.

2) ♠ 7 3 2
   ♡ Q 4
   ◇ A 6
   ♣ A Q 10 8 7 3

West	North	East	South
1◇	?		

Two clubs. With 12 HCPs and a good six-card suit you have plenty to overcall, even at the two-level.

3) ♠ A J 4
   ♡ Q 6 2
   ◇ A J 4
   ♣ K J 10 7

West	North	East	South
1◇	?		

1NT. This shows 15–17 HCPs, a balanced hand, and a good diamond stopper — exactly what you have. 1NT would be the best bid whichever suit has been opened.

4) ♠ A Q 4
   ♡ K 6 2
   ◇ 1 0 7 4
   ♣ A K 10 7

West	North	East	South
1◇	?		

Double. You have the strength and shape for a 1NT overcall but have no diamond stopper, so must look for an alternative. The shape is far from ideal, but the only possibility is a take-out double and at least you have extra high card strength to compensate for the lack of distribution.

5) ♠ A K J 6 3 2

	West	North	East	South
	1◇	?		

♡ K Q 2

◇ 7 3

♣ 9 4

Two spades. An excellent six-card suit and 13 HCPs make this hand far too good for a simple one spade bid. The jump overcall shows about 12–16 points and a good long suit.

6) ♠ A Q J 4

	West	North	East	South
	1◇	?		

♡ K 10 9 3

◇ 6

♣ A 8 7 2

Double. With four cards in each of the unbid suits you have the perfect shape to double. Why guess which suit to bid when you can ask partner to choose?

7) ♠ K 7 2

	West	North	East	South
	1♡	1♠	Pass	?

♡ 6 3

◇ A 10 4 3 2

♣ Q 6 2

Two spades. This shows 6–10 points and spade support. ♠K72 is ample support because the one spade overcall guarantees a reasonable five-card suit so there must be at least eight spades between the two hands.

8) ♠ 7 2

	West	North	East	South
	1♡	1♠	Pass	?

♡ J 5 4

◇ A K 10 8 6 3

♣ A 2

Two diamonds. With a fair hand but no real support for spades, why not offer an alternative, just as you would have done had partner opened one spade. Game could still be on if he has a near maximum overcall, and while two diamonds does not force him to bid again, he is encouraged to do so if he has anything to spare.

9)   ♠ J 10 4

     ♡ 6 3

     ◇ A 8 3 2

     ♣ K 6 4 2

West	North	East	South
1♡	2♣	Pass	?

Three clubs. You have 8 HCPs and excellent support. While five clubs is a long way away, it can do no harm to give partner another chance just in case he has a very good hand for his overcall.

10)   ♠ 10 9 8 3

     ♡ K J 10

     ◇ K J 4

     ♣ K 6 4

West	North	East	South
1♡	2♣	Pass	?

2NT. You have sufficient support to be able to raise partner's clubs, but with a flat hand and a solid heart stopper 2NT is more constructive. If partner does have a good hand, 3NT is much more likely to succeed than five clubs, as you have plenty of high cards but also a lot of potential losers owing to your lack of ruffing values.

11)   ♠ Q 6 3

     ♡ 7

     ◇ A 8 6 4 2

     ♣ J 10 7 2

West	North	East	South
1♡	2♠	Pass	?

Three spades. Only 7 HCPs, but ample trump support plus a singleton, so the true value is nearer to 10 points — enough to invite game opposite partner's announced 12–16 and probable six-card suit.

12)   ♠ 9 7 6 5 3 2

     ♡ J 4

     ◇ 8 6 2

     ♣ J 3

West	North	East	South
1♡	1NT	Pass	?

Two spades. Just as over a 1NT opening, so over a 1NT overcall, this shows a weak hand with a long suit and tells partner to pass. Clearly your hand is far more likely to produce tricks with spades as trumps than in no-trumps.

95

		West	North	East	South
13)	♠ 10643	1◇	Dble	Pass	?
	♡ J103				
	◇ 764				
	♣ Q83				

One spade. You have been asked to pick a suit and must do so despite the weakness of your hand. If instead you pass they will surely make one diamond doubled with ease, after all, you are weak and partner is likely to be short in diamonds, so how do you hope to stop them?

		West	North	East	South
14)	♠ J83	1◇	Dble	1♠	?
	♡ 10643				
	◇ 7632				
	♣ 94				

Pass. Now that the third hand has bid he has relieved you of the obligation to respond to the double. With such a weak hand, you should be delighted to avail yourself of the opportunity to pass.

		West	North	East	South
15)	♠ K7	1◇	Dble	Pass	?
	♡ A863				
	◇ 9432				
	♣ QJ4				

Two hearts. As you would have to bid even with no points at all, you must let partner know when you actually have a fair hand. Jumping in your suit shows 9–12 points and is the best choice on this hand.

		West	North	East	South
16)	♠ AJ64	1◇	Dble	Pass	?
	♡ AJ64				
	◇ A2				
	♣ 1093				

Two diamonds. You want to play in game, but which game will be best? Rather than guess between four hearts, four spades and 3NT, ask partner to show a suit by bidding the one thing you couldn't possibly want to have as trumps. After your cue-bid of the opponents' suit, the bidding must keep on until game is reached, giving you plenty of time to explore all the options on the way.

17)   ♠ K 10 9 6

	West	North	East	South
	1◇	Dble	Pass	1♡
	Pass	?		

♡ A J 4 3

◇ 7 2

♣ A K 3

Pass. Partner is known to have at most eight points, possibly nine, so there is no chance of game and no reason for you to bid again.

18)   ♠ K Q 10 5

	West	North	East	South
	1◇	Dble	Pass	2◇
	Pass	?		

♡ K Q 7

◇ 7

♣ K 10 9 8 3

Three clubs. Partner wishes to play in game but does not know which one, two diamonds has nothing to do with diamonds. He wants to hear your best suit so you must bid clubs first, you will probably get a chance to show your spades on the next round.

19)   ♠ A K 7 2

	West	North	East	South
	1◇	Dble	Pass	1♡
	Pass	?		

♡ A K 7 2

◇ 10 3

♣ A 9 4

Two hearts. Game is still a possibility, but only if partner is near to maximum for his one heart response. Despite your 18 points, you should make only a mild invitation via a single raise, he will then only bid on when he is very near to a maximum. If you wanted him to go on with less, you could always have jumped to three hearts to make a stronger invitation.

97

The opponents open 1NT

When an opponent opens 1NT he makes a very precise bid, giving his partner a good idea of his hand and leaving him in a good position to make the partnership's future decisions. This makes it relatively dangerous to overcall, as the third player can comfortably double you if he has good trumps and a few high cards. For this reason an overcall should usually be based on a six-card suit, or if only a five-card suit, then a hand with a bit of outside shape — i.e. 5-3-3-2 is a bad shape with which to overcall, while 5-4-3-1 or 5-5-2-1 is better. The overcaller should also have about 10 or more points. This does not make for perfect safety by any means, but should at least keep the really bad penalties to a minimum. Of course, passing can also be expensive; you may not concede the spectacular −800s but can instead lose a steady stream of points when 1NT makes and you could have made a partscore your way, if you had come in. This is very much an area where judgement is to the fore. A minimum overcall might be:

> ♠ A 7 3
> ♡ 9 6
> ♢ A J 8 7 6 3
> ♣ Q 2

With no long suit your options are to pass or to double. Here, where no suit has been bid, you cannot make a take-out double, instead the double means you have a better hand than the opener and hope to beat 1NT, if your partner has his fair share of what is left. So a double of a 12–14 1NT opening shows at least 15 HCPs or the equivalent. With a borderline hand it is worth looking to see if you have an attractive opening lead, such as a long suit or solid sequence of honour cards. If you have, then you should double, but otherwise it is better to pass, as you may be giving a trick away whichever suit you lead and the contract may go very well for declarer.

When partner doubles 1NT, you should usually pass, unless you have both a long suit and a weak hand, in which case you bid two of your suit, e.g. bid two spades with:

> ♠ 10 8 7 6 3
> ♡ J 10 4
> ♢ 9 7
> ♣ 6 3 2

The only other time you might bid would be with a very shapely hand, where you expect to make game in your own suit and are afraid of not beating 1NT by enough. In that case jump to game in your suit. Otherwise, just pass 1NT doubled and hope that, even it makes, you score well defending. Although it may look attractive to bid with all weak hands rather than let them make their doubled contract, remember that you are having to go to the two level and unless you have a long suit you could fare badly. 1NT doubled making may cost you −180, but that is still better than going two or three down doubled yourself. Sometimes you cannot get a good score; instead you must aim for the least bad one.

QUIZ NINE
The opponents open 1NT

Your right-hand opponent opens 1NT. What do you bid?

1) ♠ A Q 4
♡ J 9 7 3
◇ K J 4 2
♣ Q 6

2) ♠ K 10 8 7 3 2
♡ A K 4
◇ 7 6 3
♣ 2

3) ♠ K Q J 10 9
♡ A 7 6
◇ A 6 3
♣ 10 4

4) ♠ A J 10 4
♡ A 9 7
◇ A K J
♣ 10 6 2

Your left-hand opponent opens 1NT, your partner doubles and your right-hand opponent passes. What is your next bid?

5) ♠ Q 7 3
♡ J 10 4 2
◇ J 9 3
♣ 7 6 2

6) ♠ 8 7 5 3
♡ 7
◇ J 9 6 4 3
♣ 7 4 2

7) ♠ K J 9 7 6 3 2
♡ K 4
◇ 7 3 2
♣ 6

What is your next bid?

8) ♠ K Q 7
♡ K J 4
◇ A K 10 7
♣ K 8 3

West	North	East	South
1NT	Dble	Pass	2♡
Pass	?		

SOLUTIONS TO QUIZ NINE
The opponents open 1NT

1)   ♠ A Q 4
  ♡ J 9 7 3
  ◇ K J 4 2
  ♣ Q 6

	West	North	East	South
	1NT	?		

Pass. You have an opening bid, but there is nothing you can do over a 1NT opening. Your hand is too balanced for an overcall and not strong enough to make a penalty double.

2)   ♠ K 10 8 7 3 2
  ♡ A K 4
  ◇ 7 6 3
  ♣ 2

	West	North	East	South
	1NT	?		

Two spades. Less points than in the previous example, but this time you have a six-card suit and this makes your hand worth a bid. You could get unlucky, but an overcall should not come to too much harm.

3)   ♠ K Q J 10 9
  ♡ A 7 6
  ◇ A 6 3
  ♣ 10 4

	West	North	East	South
	1NT	?		

Double. Your first instinct will be to overcall two spades because you have a good five-card suit and 14 HCPs, but a little more thought might make you change your mind. If you lead a spade against 1NT, you will set up six defensive tricks immediately, so you need very little help from partner to beat 1NT. Indeed, one trick will do, while you would need two to make two spades.

4)   ♠ A J 10 4
  ♡ A 9 7
  ◇ A K J
  ♣ 10 6 2

	West	North	East	South
	1NT	?		

Double. This is the more common type of double, a balanced hand with greater strength than the opener. Despite the 17 HCPs, you will actually need more help from your partner than on the previous hand. The lack of a good suit to lead is a serious handicap.

		West	North	East	South
5)	♠ Q73	West	North	East	South
	♡ J1042	1NT	Dble	Pass	?
	◇ J93				
	♣ 762				

Pass. If partner is minimum for his double, this could be very close to making, but with your flat hand, you have no way of knowing if anything else will be better. Best is to pass and hope that what little you have will prove to be sufficient to beat 1NT, more often than not it will be.

		West	North	East	South
6)	♠ 8753	West	North	East	South
	♡ 7	1NT	Dble	Pass	?
	◇ J9643				
	♣ 742				

Two diamonds. This hand is even weaker than the last example, so you are really worried about the possibility of 1NT doubled making. Fortunately, you have a bit of shape so can afford to bid. The position is similar to that when partner has opened 1NT, in which case you would have bid two diamonds as a weak take-out, because you rate to make more tricks with your hand if diamonds are trumps than in no-trumps.

		West	North	East	South
7)	♠ KJ97632	West	North	East	South
	♡ K4	1NT	Dble	Pass	?
	◇ 732				
	♣ 6				

Four spades. You have plenty of strength with which to pass, but your very long suit suggests that spades really should be trumps. Opposite a flattish 15 plus HCPs it is almost certain that you can make game, while 1NT doubled may not go many down, if at all, because partner is most unlikely ever to lead spades, as he cannot have many of them. Meanwhile declarer may be able to run four or five tricks in another suit — probably clubs.

		West	North	East	South
8)	♠ KQ7	West	North	East	South
	♡ KJ4	1NT	Dble	Pass	2♡
	◇ AK107	Pass	?		
	♣ J83				

Pass. Partner has shown a weak hand with five or more hearts. He does not want to hear another bid from you unless you have an exceptional hand. As this is just an average doubling hand, you should pass and hope that he can scramble eight tricks.

The opponents open with three of a suit

Given that it can be hard enough to reach the right contract even when given a completely free run, you can imagine how difficult it can become when an opponent bids at the three level, before either you or your partner has had an opportunity to speak. The whole point of pre-empting is to make life difficult for the opposition and to make them guess, and inevitably you will not guess right all the time — the best you can do is to follow the rules and keep your fingers crossed.

Bids over an opposing pre-empt mean much the same as over a one-level opening. In other words, an overcall shows a good long suit, double is for take-out, and a no-trump bid shows a fairly balanced hand with a good stopper in the opponent's suit. Because you are starting two levels higher, however, you need a little extra strength.

An overcall shows a hand with a six-card or very good five-card suit, which would have opened the bidding, say 12 plus HCPs with six cards, 14 plus with five cards. If you have a very strong hand with a six-card or longer suit, 19 or 20 HCPs upwards, so that you need very little help from partner to make a game, you should jump to game yourself, e.g. bid four spades over three clubs with:

♠ A K J 10 8 7
♡ A K Q
♢ Q 3
♣ 10 7

It is not that you are totally confident of making four spades, but if you bid only three spades, partner will pass far too often when he has sufficient bits and pieces for you but he fears that you have a much weaker hand, say:

♠ A K J 6 3 2
♡ A 4 2
♢ 7 3
♣ J 6

A take-out double should show about 14 plus HCPs and support for the unbid suits. As usual, the less ideal your distribution the more high-card strength is needed in compensation, e.g. double three clubs with:

♠ A Q 6 4
♡ K Q 3
◇ A J 7 4
♣ 8 2

A 3NT overcall requires around 17+ HCPs but may be bid on a little less
if you hold a long suit as a potential source of tricks. The same bid may
also be made on a good deal more than that, after all partner may have
very little and, while risks sometimes have to be taken to avoid being talked
out of a good game, you will sometimes have enough strength to feel fairly
confident. Bid 3NT over three clubs with:

♠ A Q 7 3		♠ A 3
♡ A J 5	or	♡ K J 5
◇ K 9 4		◇ K Q 10 9 6 3
♣ K J 8		♣ A Q

The general rule is that when deciding whether or not to bid, you assume
partner has about seven or eight points and bid (or not) accordingly. Of
course he may not have so much, but you have to make some assumption.
The other side of the coin is that when partner overcalls or doubles a three
opening, you should discount the first seven or eight points in your hand,
on the assumption that partner has already allowed for them and should
only bid on if you have even more than that. With less than seven or eight
points then, you should pass partner's overcall and respond as cheaply as
possible to his take-out double. With much more than seven or eight, however, you should bid game, usually by supporting his suit or bidding 3NT,
or jumping in your suit over a double.

The most important thing when somebody pre-empts against you is just to
accept that you are in an awkward position and will not always reach the
perfect contract. You should always aim to achieve a sensible result even
if it is not the best, rather than strive for perfection and risk something
ridiculous happening. In other words, settle for the best result possible
rather than the best possible result.

QUIZ TEN
The opponents open at the three level

Your right-hand opponent opens three clubs. What do you bid?

1) ♠ K 108732
    ♡ A Q 6
    ◇ J 7
    ♣ 10 3

2) ♠ A K 3
    ♡ A Q J 643
    ◇ 73
    ♣ 10 4

3) ♠ A K 3
    ♡ A Q J 10874
    ◇ Q 2
    ♣ 5

Your right-hand opponent opens three spades. What do you bid?

4) ♠ 6
    ♡ K 32
    ◇ A K 6
    ♣ K Q 8764

5) ♠ 73
    ♡ A Q J 4
    ◇ K 1087
    ♣ A K 3

6) ♠ A Q
    ♡ K J 3
    ◇ A 4
    ♣ K Q 10964

What is your next bid?

7) ♠ J 73
    ♡ Q 64
    ◇ A 1083
    ♣ 652

West	North	East	South
3♣	3♡	Pass	?

8) ♠ J 10732
    ♡ Q 104
    ◇ A 832
    ♣ 7

West	North	East	South
3♣	3♡	Pass	?

9) ♠ Q 864
    ♡ 73
    ◇ A J 10
    ♣ K 1094

West	North	East	South
3♣	3♡	Pass	?

10) ♠ Q 632
    ♡ J 1042
    ◇ 963
    ♣ Q 2

West	North	East	South
3♣	Dble	Pass	?

105

		West	North	East	South
11)	♠ KQ98 ♡ J103 ◇ A862 ♣ 104	3♣	Dble	Pass	?
12)	♠ A83 ♡ K94 ◇ 1063 ♣ QJ108	3♣	Dble	Pass	?
13)	♠ AJ83 ♡ AQ64 ◇ KJ95 ♣ 10	3♣ Pass	Dble ?	Pass	3♡
14)	♠ AK83 ♡ AQ64 ◇ AQ109 ♣ 8	3♣ Pass	Dble ?	Pass	3♡
15)	♠ AJ83 ♡ AQ64 ◇ KJ95 ♣ 3	3♣ Pass	Dble ?	Pass	3NT

SOLUTIONS TO QUIZ TEN

The opponents open at the three level

		West	North	East	South
1)	♠ K 10 8 7 3 2	West	North	East	South
	♡ A Q 6	3♣	?		
	◇ J 7				
	♣ 10 3				

Pass. You would have bid one spade over one club, but are about a king short of having an overcall at the three-level.

		West	North	East	South
2)	♠ A K 3	West	North	East	South
	♡ A Q J 6 4 3	3♣	?		
	◇ 7 3				
	♣ 10 4				

Three hearts. A good six-card suit and 14 HCPs is a sound overcall even at the three-level. You might just make the same bid with a heart less.

		West	North	East	South
3)	♠ A K 3	West	North	East	South
	♡ A Q J 10 8 7 4	3♣	?		
	◇ Q 2				
	♣ 5				

Four hearts. You do not, of course, have ten tricks, but need so little from partner that, even if he has it, he may pass and you will miss the game. Take the pressure off him by jumping to game yourself.

		West	North	East	South
4)	♠ 6	West	North	East	South
	♡ K 3 2	3♠	?		
	◇ A K 6				
	♣ K Q 8 7 6 4				

Four clubs. Not a lot to spare for an overcall at this level, but the six-card suit makes it worth the risk. Although you are short in spades, it is better to bid your long suit rather than double as you have a strong preference for clubs. Partner, with enough strength for game, can always introduce a red suit of five cards or more, if he wishes.

107

5)	♠ 73	**West**	**North**	**East**	**South**
	♡ A Q J 4	3♠	?		
	◇ K 10 8 7				
	♣ A K 3				

Double. There is nothing you can overcall, yet with so many high cards you clearly must bid something. Double, asking partner to pick a suit, fits the bill nicely.

6)	♠ A Q	**West**	**North**	**East**	**South**
	♡ K J 3	3♠	?		
	◇ A 4				
	♣ K Q 10 9 6 4				

3NT. First thoughts might be to bid the clubs, but with a high card in every suit, including a double stop in spades, it may prove easier to make nine tricks in no-trumps than ten in clubs — and, of course, you score far more if you do succeed in no-trumps.

7)	♠ J 7 3	**West**	**North**	**East**	**South**
	♡ Q 6 4	3♣	3♡	Pass	?
	◇ A 10 8 3				
	♣ 6 5 2				

Pass. Partner has not shown nine tricks by bidding three hearts, he has said that he hopes to make nine tricks if you have a little help for him. He has assumed seven or eight points in your hand and you should only bid on if you have more than that.

8)	♠ J 10 7 3 2	**West**	**North**	**East**	**South**
	♡ Q 10 4	3♣	3♡	Pass	?
	◇ A 8 3 2				
	♣ 7				

Four hearts. This is by no means a certainty, but this time you not only have 7 HCPs, but also a useful looking singleton, so game should make a fair proportion of the time.

9)	♠ Q 8 6 4	**West**	**North**	**East**	**South**
	♡ 7 3	3♣	3♡	Pass	?
	◇ A J 10				
	♣ K 10 9 4				

3NT. Close to a minimum for this response, but you do have all the suits stopped and can hope to find a good source of tricks in partner's heart suit.

		West	North	East	South
10)	♠ Q632 ♡ J1042 ◇ 963 ♣ Q2	3♣	Dble	Pass	?

Three hearts. You must bid even with a weak hand, and with two four-card suits you should choose the cheaper one, as partner may occasionally bid three spades over three hearts but will rarely consider bidding four hearts over three spades.

		West	North	East	South
11)	♠ KQ98 ♡ J103 ◇ A862 ♣ 104	3♣	Dble	Pass	?

Four spades. With 10 HCPs, you must jump to game to give partner the good news, and clearly the major is the suit to bid, as four spades requires a trick less than five diamonds. It is essential to jump, as otherwise partner will be left guessing how strong you are. After all, you could bid three spades with nothing.

		West	North	East	South
12)	♠ A83 ♡ K94 ◇ 1063 ♣ QJ108	3♣	Dble	Pass	?

Pass. With good clubs you can pass and take the sure profit. Partner's high cards plus your two trump tricks should be sufficient to get three clubs doubled at least three down.

		West	North	East	South
13)	♠ AJ83 ♡ AQ64 ◇ KJ95 ♣ 10	3♣ Pass	Dble ?	Pass	3♡

Pass. As partner did not jump he is known to be weak, so with little to spare for your double you have no reason to bid again. Note the importance of knowing that he is weak; without that information you would be guessing what to do.

14) ♠ A K 8 3

	West	North	East	South
	3♣	Dble	Pass	3♡
	Pass	?		

♡ A Q 6 4
◇ A Q 10 9
♣ 8

Four hearts. Again, partner is known to be weak, but this time you have a good deal to spare so can risk a raise. He will not need to have very much, but even with your powerful hand four hearts is by no means a certainty, as he could have absolutely nothing.

15) ♠ A J 8 3

	West	North	East	South
	3♣	Dble	Pass	3NT
	Pass	?		

♡ A Q 6 4
◇ K J 9 5
♣ 3

Pass. You asked partner to pick a suit and he has chosen no-trumps instead. You may not like no-trumps, but you have exactly the sort of hand partner will be expecting, so you should trust him to know what he is doing.

SECTION THREE
WE OPEN THE BIDDING, THEY INTERVENE

The opponents overcall

An opposing overcall does not make a huge difference to your bidding. The two main changes are as follows:

Firstly, you must never be the first person to bid no-trumps unless you have a sure stopper in the overcaller's suit. He has promised at least a five-card suit, and for sure that is the suit they are going to lead. Obviously you don't want to start by losing the first five or six tricks, so if you do bid no-trumps, you must have a high card to stop them running the suit against you.

Secondly, whilst you are normally expected to find some response to a suit opening whenever you have six or more points, once the opposition intervene, you are entitled to pass if there is nothing you want to say — indeed, you may sometimes have no option, e.g. the bidding goes 1◇ – 1♠ – ? You hold:

♠ 8 7 3
♡ J 7 6 3 2
◇ A 4
♣ J 5 2

and you are not strong enough to bid a new suit at the two level, cannot support diamonds, and cannot bid no-trumps with no spade stopper, so you have no choice but to pass. However, after 1◇ – 1♡ – ? you should bid one spade on:

♠ J 7 6 3 2
♡ 8 7 3
◇ A 4
♣ J 5 2

because you are strong enough to bid a new suit at the one level. And after 1◇ – 1♠ – ? you could bid two diamonds with:

111

♠ 7 3
♡ A J 6 4
♢ K 7 3
♣ 8 6 4 2

Your useful doubleton and near maximum in high cards should compensate for the missing fourth trump — you need to be a little more flexible when both sides are bidding, or you will get shut out far too often.

The other main change when there has been an overcall is that you have a new option, namely to double. So far we have only really looked at the double as a way of getting partner to speak, but this take-out meaning only applies when the double was your side's first positive bid during the auction. Otherwise, as here, it is for penalties, telling partner that you expect to beat the opposing contract and want to increase the penalty. So 1♢ – 1♠ – Double is for penalties and might be bid with a hand such as:

♠ A J 10 8 6
♡ A 4 3
♢ 7
♣ J 10 9 4

It is important that you hold good trumps, not just high cards, as otherwise the penalty, if any, may prove disappointing.

Where an opponent overcalls 1NT, a double is still for penalties and simply means that you think your side has the majority of the high cards. If you have a long suit, you may bid it at the two level instead. This tells partner that unless he has extra strength, you do not have sufficient for game but you wish to compete for the part-score. You do not compel him to bid again if he does not wish to do so.

QUIZ ELEVEN
The opponents overcall

Your partner opens one diamond and your right-hand opponent overcalls one spade. What do you bid?

1) ♠ 732
  ♡ A4
  ◇ KJ86
  ♣ QJ32

2) ♠ Q105
  ♡ A43
  ◇ K32
  ♣ 6432

3) ♠ 1064
  ♡ A8752
  ◇ 73
  ♣ K64

4) ♠ 1064
  ♡ AQ1064
  ◇ 82
  ♣ K64

Your partner opens one club and your right-hand opponent overcalls one heart. What do you bid?

5) ♠ Q1064
  ♡ A4
  ◇ J932
  ♣ 876

6) ♠ Q64
  ♡ J32
  ◇ Q10743
  ♣ Q6

7) ♠ K83
  ♡ K7
  ◇ J9753
  ♣ 642

8) ♠ J83
  ♡ KJ985
  ◇ A74
  ♣ 62

Your partner opens one heart and your right-hand opponent overcalls two clubs. What do you bid?

9) ♠ J10732
  ♡ K76
  ◇ 82
  ♣ K108

10) ♠ K103
  ♡ K64
  ◇ QJ92
  ♣ K108

11) ♠ K432
♡ QJ72
◇ K832
♣ 6

12) ♠ J873
♡ 7
◇ AQ65
♣ K1083

13) ♠ 964
♡ 72
◇ J83
♣ QJ1074

14) ♠ 1094
♡ J8
◇ AQ642
♣ A53

Your partner opens one heart and your right-hand opponent overcalls 1NT. What do you bid?

15) ♠ A87
♡ K5
◇ Q1064
♣ J873

SOLUTIONS TO QUIZ ELEVEN
The opponents overcall

1) ♠ 732
    ♡ A 4
    ◇ K J 8 6
    ♣ Q J 3 2

West	North	East	South
1◇	1♠	?	

Three diamonds. Just as you would have bid without the overcall, showing four-card support and 10–12 points.

2) ♠ Q 10 5
    ♡ A 4 3
    ◇ K 3 2
    ♣ 6 4 3 2

West	North	East	South
1◇	1♠	?	

1NT. This shows 6–9 points and a balanced hand, but also guarantees a spade stopper. The stopper, ♠Q105, is not quite a sure one, but you are absolutely maximum and really must try to find some bid with 9 HCPs.

3) ♠ 1064
    ♡ A 8 7 5 2
    ◇ 7 3
    ♣ K 6 4

West	North	East	South
1◇	1♠	?	

Pass. You cannot support diamonds on two small, cannot bid no-trumps with no spade stopper, and do not have the 9 or more HCPs required to bid a new suit at the two level. There is no need to worry. The main reason why you usually have to respond on as few as six or seven points is to give partner a second chance in case he is very strong. Here, he will get another chance anyway, whether or not you bid.

4) ♠ 1064
    ♡ A Q 10 6 4
    ◇ 8 2
    ♣ K 6 4

West	North	East	South
1◇	1♠	?	

Two hearts. This time you have 9 HCPs plus a five-card suit, just enough for a new suit response at the two-level.

5)	♠ Q1064	**West**	**North**	**East**	**South**
	♡ A4	1♣	1♡	?	
	◇ J932				
	♣ 876				

One spade. A new suit should still be bid at the one-level with six or more points where possible. You could also consider bidding no-trumps, as you do have the hearts stopped, but just as in an uncontested auction, a four-card suit at the one-level should take precedence in case partner also has four.

6)	♠ Q64	**West**	**North**	**East**	**South**
	♡ J32	1♣	1♡	?	
	◇ Q10743				
	♣ Q6				

Pass. You are not strong enough for two diamonds, cannot support clubs, and have no heart stopper, so you have no option.

7)	♠ K83	**West**	**North**	**East**	**South**
	♡ K7	1♣	1♡	?	
	◇ J9753				
	♣ 642				

1NT. Now you do have the heart stopper, you can bid no-trumps, showing your point count, 6–9, in the process.

8)	♠ J83	**West**	**North**	**East**	**South**
	♡ KJ985	1♣	1♡	?	
	◇ A74				
	♣ 62				

Double. You have excellent trumps sitting over the overcaller and can hope to beat one heart pretty easily, unless partner has an unusual hand, in which case he can overrule your decision and remove the double, e.g. with:

♠ A 10 7 4 2
♡ 6
◇ 5
♣ A Q J 7 4 3

he would bid one spade, because he would be *very* keen to have one of his suits as trumps.

9) ♠ J 10 7 3 2
    ♡ K 7 6
    ◇ 8 2
    ♣ K 10 8

West	North	East	South
1♡	2♣	?	

Two hearts. You are not strong enough for two spades and your clubs are well short of what is required for a double. Three reasonable hearts plus a ruffing value (the doubleton diamond) make this worth a raise to two hearts.

10) ♠ K 10 3
    ♡ K 6 4
    ◇ Q J 9 2
    ♣ K 10 8

West	North	East	South
1♡	2♣	?	

2NT. You could bid two diamonds, but the all-round nature of your hand is better expressed by a bid in no-trumps, 2NT showing 11 or 12 HCPs with a sure club stop.

11) ♠ K 4 3 2
    ♡ Q J 7 2
    ◇ K 8 3 2
    ♣ 6

West	North	East	South
1♡	2♣	?	

Three hearts. This shows 10–12 points and four-card support, just as if the overcall had not occurred. Don't forget to add points for the singleton now that you have found a fit.

12) ♠ J 8 7 3
    ♡ 7
    ◇ A Q 6 5
    ♣ K 10 8 3

West	North	East	South
1♡	2♣	?	

Double. You probably have two trump tricks anyway, but the shortage in partner's suit suggests that you might make more by trumping hearts. A shortage in partner's suit is always a big plus when considering doubling your opponents for just that reason, and with your side having the edge in high cards as well, you can expect to do very well against two clubs. As there is no guarantee that you could make a game your way, what better time to defend and pick up a big fat penalty?

13) ♠ 9 6 4
♡ 7 2
♢ J 8 3
♣ Q J 10 7 4

West	North	East	South
1♡	2♣	?	

Pass. With three sure trump tricks it may look obvious to double as you expect to beat two clubs. The problem comes, however, when you double and they run to somewhere else. Now your partner may double, expecting you to have some high cards, and may have great difficulty in beating their contract when you fail to produce the goods. The trouble is your hand is *only* useful against clubs, so be happy to have them where you want them and settle for a sure plus score rather than risk frightening them away.

14) ♠ 1 0 9 4
♡ J 8
♢ A Q 6 4 2
♣ A 5 3

West	North	East	South
1♡	2♣	?	

Two diamonds. You do have a club stopper, so could bid no-trumps, but why not show your suit first? After all, you can always bid no-trumps next time round, can't you? This way you give partner a choice, which he would not have if you bid 2NT straightaway.

15) ♠ A 8 7
♡ K 5
♢ Q 10 6 4
♣ J 8 7 3

West	North	East	South
1♡	1NT	?	

Double. You know that your side has the balance of points. Double to suggest to partner that you defend and hopefully collect a nice penalty. Partner will only remove the double if he is very shapely and thinks that the hand will be better played in one of his suits.

The opponents double

When partner opens with one of a suit and the next hand doubles, there is no point in thinking to yourself, "I've got a good hand and I like partner's suit, so I'll pass, because he should make it easily", because, of course, the double is for take-out and you will never actually be left to play there. Generally speaking, the rules of bidding are pretty much the same as though the double had not occurred, i.e. a new suit shows 6 plus HCPs at the one level and 9 plus HCPs at the two level, and raises of partner's suit are limit bids showing the value of your hand. There are a few differences, however.

Firstly, when the bidding commences 1◇ – Double – ?, the doubler has shown interest in all the other suits apart from diamonds, so there is probably not much point in your bidding a weak four-card suit, which is quite likely to be breaking badly even if partner does have a fit for it. With, say:

> ♠ K 7 6 3
> ♡ Q 4 2
> ◇ J 7 3
> ♣ J 8 4

there is a good case for just bidding 1NT (6–9) and forgetting about the spades. On the other hand, bid one spade with:

> ♠ A Q J 4
> ♡ J 3 2
> ◇ 7 6 4
> ♣ 8 5 2

because the suit is strong — you want partner to lead a spade if they outbid you, while if it ends up as your trump suit, its strength should leave you in a reasonable position to overcome any bad break.

Secondly, if you have a fit for partner's suit you should strain to support him to as high a level as you can straightaway. Why? If one side has a fit in one suit the other side is bound to have a fit somewhere else, if only they can find it. The more you bid, the harder you make it for them to find their fit and the more likely you are to buy the contract. In the final section of this book we will look at this situation in more detail. For the moment, if you just choose the higher of two bids whenever you have a borderline decision, you will make life that little bit more difficult for the opposition — always a good thing.

You also have an extra option, you can redouble. If that ended the auction, i.e. everybody passed, it would just mean that the scores were multiplied by four instead of two, but of course the double was for take-out, so normally someone will bid. A redouble does not simply mean that you expect partner to make his contract, as we have already seen there would be little point in that. Instead, it is used to tell partner that your side has the majority of the high cards and that you might be interested in trying to penalise the opposition. You promised 9 or more HCPs and are usually either fairly balanced or are short in partner's suit but have the other three. If you had genuine support for partner, you would raise him, while with a long suit of your own, you would just bid it. Really you are asking partner to co-operate by doubling the opposition if he holds their suit and, if not, to give you the chance to do so when you have it. The only time he should actually bid something himself is if he has a weakish shapely hand with which he has no interest in defending. After 1◇ – Double – Redouble - ? he can even pass and be sure that you will say something. It would not make much sense to let them play at the one level, when you have the majority of the points, would it? At least not unless you are going to double them. So obvious is this, that it is a rule that once your side has redoubled, one of you must bid again, rather than let the opposition play undoubled at the one or two level. If you do not wish to commit yourself you can always pass and leave the decision to your partner. He *must* now do something, i.e. the pass is forcing on him.

QUIZ TWELVE
The opponents double

Your partner opens one diamond and your right-hand opponent makes a take-out double. What do you bid?

1) ♠ 874
   ♡ Q986
   ◇ Q43
   ♣ K107

2) ♠ 8742
   ♡ 76
   ◇ Q986
   ♣ K107

3) ♠ KJ1075
   ♡ 103
   ◇ A54
   ♣ 976

4) ♠ A82
   ♡ QJ84
   ◇ K3
   ♣ J1084

5) ♠ AK43
   ♡ 72
   ◇ J86
   ♣ 10932

6) ♠ Q64
   ♡ 76
   ◇ K3
   ♣ AK8742

7) ♠ 862
   ♡ 104
   ◇ K1086
   ♣ AQ73

What do you bid next?

8) ♠ 76
   ♡ AJ84
   ◇ AQ732
   ♣ K2

West	North	East	South
1◇	Dble	Rdble	1♡
?			

9) ♠ AJ84
   ♡ 76
   ◇ AQ732
   ♣ K2

West	North	East	South
1◇	Dble	Rdble	1♡
?			

10) ♠ 1094
     ♡ K7
     ◇ KQ10873
     ♣ K2

West	North	East	South
1◇	Dble	Rdble	1♡
?			

11) ♠ AJ732
     ♡ 10
     ◇ KQJ642
     ♣ 7

West	North	East	South
1◇	Dble	Rdble	1♡
?			

12) ♠ J6
     ♡ K4
     ◇ AKQJ873
     ♣ 103

West	North	East	South
1◇	Dble	Rdble	1♡
?			

13) ♠ Q72
     ♡ KJ98
     ◇ A3
     ♣ J742

West	North	East	South
1◇	Dble	Rdble	1♡
Pass	Pass	?	

14) ♠ AJ42
     ♡ 732
     ◇ K86
     ♣ Q72

West	North	East	South
1◇	Dble	Rdble	1♡
Pass	Pass	?	

15) ♠ K97
     ♡ Q102
     ◇ 832
     ♣ AJ42

West	North	East	South
1◇	Dble	Rdble	1♡
Pass	Pass	?	

SOLUTIONS TO QUIZ TWELVE
The opponents double

1) ♠ 874
   ♡ Q986
   ◇ Q43
   ♣ K107

West	North	East	South
1◇	Dble	?	

1NT. This shows a balanced hand of 6–9 HCPs, just what you have. Without the double, you would have shown your four-card heart suit, but it is quite weak and probably not worth bidding now that the doubler has shown an interest in hearts.

2) ♠ 8742
   ♡ 76
   ◇ Q986
   ♣ K107

West	North	East	South
1◇	Dble	?	

Two diamonds. Minimum, but worth a slight stretch to make life more difficult for the opposition. Remember, you will not be left in one diamond doubled, so there is no point in passing just because you expect that contract to make.

3) ♠ KJ1075
   ♡ 103
   ◇ A54
   ♣ 976

West	North	East	South
1◇	Dble	?	

One spade. With a good five-card suit you just make your normal response, as though the double had not happened.

4) ♠ A82
   ♡ QJ84
   ◇ K3
   ♣ J1084

West	North	East	South
1◇	Dble	?	

Redouble. Knowing that your side has a clear majority of the points, and having no great liking for partner's suit, you are more interested in trying to penalise the opposition than in playing the hand yourself. When one side has a fit, so does the other, as we have already seen. The other side of the coin is that, if one side does NOT have a fit, then usually neither does the other, so they could be in trouble, depending on just what sort of hand partner actually has.

			West	North	East	South
5)	♠	A K 4 3	1◇	Dble	?	
	♡	72				
	◇	J 8 6				
	♣	10 9 3 2				

One spade. This time, although your hand is balanced, most of its high-card strength is in the four-card spade suit, so it is better to show your suit rather than bid 1NT, as you might have done had the high cards been more scattered.

			West	North	East	South
6)	♠	Q 6 4	1◇	Dble	?	
	♡	76				
	◇	K 3				
	♣	A K 8 7 4 2				

Two clubs. Though you are strong enough to redouble, you have no great interest in defending, even against a doubled contract, as surely they will have a fit in one of the majors. Much better is to describe your own hand to partner by bidding your long suit.

			West	North	East	South
7)	♠	862	1◇	Dble	?	
	♡	104				
	◇	K 10 8 6				
	♣	A Q 7 3				

Three diamonds. With good four-card support, you must raise partner's suit. Again, there is no point in redoubling, as you have no interest in defending. Without the double, it would have been touch and go whether to raise to two diamonds or three diamonds. Following the general principle of making life as tough as possible for your opponents, however, you should certainly stretch to three diamonds over the double. Partner should not get carried away by this, as he should be aware that you might be stretching a little.

			West	North	East	South
8)	♠	76	1◇	Dble	Rdble	1♡
	♡	A J 8 4	?			
	◇	A Q 7 3 2				
	♣	K 2				

Double. Partner has invited you to co-operate in penalising the opposition and with such good hearts you should be delighted to do so.

9)   ♠ A J 8 4

    ♡ 7 6

    ♢ A Q 7 3 2

    ♣ K 2

West	North	East	South
1♢	Dble	Rdble	1♡
?			

Pass. Though you cannot double one heart yourself, you have a reasonable defensive hand and would be quite happy to hear partner double. Passing gives him the opportunity to do so, and if instead he makes some other bid, you have lost nothing. Remember, partner must do something, he cannot just pass one heart out.

10) ♠ 1 0 9 4

    ♡ K 7

    ♢ K Q 10 8 7 3

    ♣ K 2

West	North	East	South
1♢	Dble	Rdble	1♡
?			

Two diamonds. You only opened this hand because of the long suit, and have no interest in defending. Just rebid your diamonds to show a minimum hand with a long suit.

11) ♠ A J 7 3 2

    ♡ 10

    ♢ K Q J 6 4 2

    ♣ 7

West	North	East	South
1♢	Dble	Rdble	1♡
?			

One spade. Again you have a shapely hand and do not wish to defend but want to make sure that one of your suits becomes trumps. Bid one spade and partner will know you have a weakish two-suiter, as with a stronger hand you could have jumped in your second suit.

12) ♠ J 6

    ♡ K 4

    ♢ A K Q J 8 7 3

    ♣ 10 3

West	North	East	South
1♢	Dble	Rdble	1♡
?			

3NT. Not an obvious bid at first sight, I must admit, but you have a very powerful suit which will provide a source of tricks and partner has shown enough high-card strength to probably cover the other three suits. Clearly, with nearly all your strength in diamonds, you have no interest in defending, while 3NT is likely to prove much easier to make than five diamonds.

13)	♠ Q72	West	North	East	South
	♡ KJ98	1♢	Dble	Rdble	1♡
	♢ A3	Pass	Pass	?	
	♣ J742				

Double. You have good hearts, so should try to penalise your opponents. Partner may have passed solely to give you the opportunity to do so.

14)	♠ AJ42	West	North	East	South
	♡ 732	1♢	Dble	Rdble	1♡
	♢ K86	Pass	Pass	?	
	♣ Q72				

One spade. With only three small hearts, you can hardly double, yet you must do something. Partner will not expect you to have a long spade suit, as you would then have bid it straightaway rather than redouble.

15)	♠ K97	West	North	East	South
	♡ Q102	1♢	Dble	Rdble	1♡
	♢ 832	Pass	Pass	?	
	♣ AJ42				

1NT. You could risk a double, but the hearts are barely adequate and it could go badly wrong. Better is to show your balanced hand, heart stopper, and minimum redouble by bidding 1NT. With more you would jump to 2NT or 3NT.

PUTTING IT ALL TOGETHER
Revision Quiz One

What is your opening bid?

1) ♠ A Q 7 3
  ♡ A J 4 2
  ◇ K 10 6 3
  ♣ 7

2) ♠ J 7 6 3 2
  ♡ A K Q J
  ◇ 7
  ♣ Q 6 3

3) ♠ A J 7 6 2
  ♡ K 4
  ◇ 8
  ♣ A J 7 6 2

Your partner opens one diamond. What do you respond?

4) ♠ Q 7 3 2
  ♡ 8
  ◇ 6 4
  ♣ A 10 9 6 4 3

5) ♠ A J 7 3 2
  ♡ K Q 5
  ◇ 8 3
  ♣ K 6 2

6) ♠ Q 9 2
  ♡ 10 7
  ◇ Q 7 6 4
  ♣ A K 6 3

Your partner opens one heart. What do you respond?

7) ♠ Q 10 7 4
  ♡ 8 6
  ◇ A Q J 4 2
  ♣ 7 3

8) ♠ Q 10 6 5
  ♡ A 3
  ◇ A K 7 6 5
  ♣ 9 4

9) ♠ Q 10 7 4
  ♡ A K 9 5 2
  ◇ A 6
  ♣ 7 3

West	East
1♡	2♣
?	

10) ♠ A Q 10 7
  ♡ A K 9 5 2
  ◇ A 6
  ♣ 7 3

West	East
1♡	2♣
?	

11) ♠ A J 10 7 3
  ♡ A Q 7
  ◇ A Q 2
  ♣ 6 4

West	East
1♠	2♠
?	

			West	East
12)	♠	A 4	**West**	**East**
	♡	A Q 10 8 5	1♡	1NT
	◇	A K J 8 7	?	
	♣	10		

			West	East
13)	♠	K 10 7 3	**West**	**East**
	♡	A Q J 6 4	1♡	1♠
	◇	A Q	?	
	♣	9 4		

			West	East
14)	♠	A Q 4	**West**	**East**
	♡	J 10 7 5	1♡	1♠
	◇	A K 7	?	
	♣	Q 6 3		

			West	East
15)	♠	K 3	**West**	**East**
	♡	Q J 6 4	1♡	2♡
	◇	10 8 6 4	3♡	?
	♣	9 7 3		

			West	East
16)	♠	A K 3	**West**	**East**
	♡	10 5 4 2	1♡	2♡
	◇	J 10 9 4	3♡	?
	♣	7 6		

			West	East
17)	♠	7 4	**West**	**East**
	♡	J 3 2	1♠	1NT
	◇	K J 7 3	2♣	?
	♣	A 7 3 2		

			West	East
18)	♠	J 3	**West**	**East**
	♡	K Q 4 2	1♠	1NT
	◇	10 7 6 4 3	2♣	?
	♣	J 3		

			West	East
19)	♠	7	**West**	**East**
	♡	K 6 3	1♠	2♣
	◇	J 10 7 4	2♡	?
	♣	A J 10 9 7		

			West	East
20)	♠	Q 4	**West**	**East**
	♡	J 6 4	1♠	2♣
	◇	K Q 4	2♡	?
	♣	K 10 9 7 5		

Putting it all together

21)	♠ KJ3 ♡ A4 ◇ 762 ♣ K9863	**West** 1♠ 2♡	**East** 2♣ ?		
22)	♠ QJ3 ♡ 10 ◇ J1097 ♣ AJ1097	**West** 1♡ 2♠	**East** 2♣ ?		
23)	♠ A4 ♡ KJ3 ◇ 1063 ♣ AJ873	**West** 1♡ 2♠	**East** 2♣ ?		
24)	♠ AQ64 ♡ AK1073 ◇ 86 ♣ A4	**West** 1♡ 2♠ ?	**East** 2♣ 2NT		
25)	♠ AK65 ♡ AJ1094 ◇ 10 ♣ A83	**West** 1♡ 2♠ ?	**East** 2♣ 2NT		
26)	♠ J4 ♡ AQ32 ◇ K764 ♣ K103	**West** 1NT ?	**East** 2♠		
27)	♠ A4 ♡ KJ54 ◇ J97 ♣ AJ62	**West** 1NT ?	**East** 2NT		
28)	♠ QJ73 ♡ 6 ◇ K642 ♣ J832	**West** 1♡ 2♡	**East** 1♠ ?		
29)	♠ AJ32 ♡ K97 ◇ 8 ♣ Q10643	**West** 1◇	**North** 1♠	**East** Pass	**South** ?

30) ♠ Q 10 7 3
    ♡ 8 4
    ◇ K Q 5
    ♣ Q J 8 7

West	North	East	South
1♡	1NT	Pass	?

31) ♠ 1 0 5 4
    ♡ Q 7 6 3
    ◇ A J 5 2
    ♣ 7 4

West	North	East	South
1♣	1♠	?	

32) ♠ K 4
    ♡ J 7 3 2
    ◇ Q J 6 3
    ♣ 1 0 9 4

West	North	East	South
1♡	1♠	?	

33) ♠ 8
    ♡ J 10 6 3
    ◇ K Q J 4
    ♣ 7 4 3 2

West	North	East	South
1♡	Dble	?	

Solutions to Revision Quiz One

What do you open?

1) ♠ A Q 7 3
   ♡ A J 4 2
   ◇ K 10 6 3
   ♣ 7

One heart. With three touching suits, open the middle one. This gives the best chance of exploring possible fits in all three suits, while guaranteeing that you will always have a sensible rebid available whatever partner's response.

2) ♠ J 7 6 3 2
   ♡ A K Q J
   ◇ 7
   ♣ Q 6 3

One spade. Always bid the longer suit first, irrespective of their relative strengths.

3) ♠ A J 7 6 2
   ♡ K 4
   ◇ 8
   ♣ A J 7 6 2

One club. Normally you open the higher of two five-card suits, but clubs and spades are the exception. One club allows you to show both suits much more economically than if you start with one spade.

4) ♠ Q 7 3 2   West   East
   ♡ 8   1◇   ?
   ◇ 6 4
   ♣ A 10 9 6 4 3

One spade. Although clubs are your longest suit, you are not strong enough to bid a new suit at the two level (9 plus HCPs) so must look for an alternative. Fortunately you have a four-card spade suit, and a new suit at the one level only requires 6 plus HCPs.

131

5)   ♠ A J 7 3 2   **West**   **East**
      ♡ K Q 5   1◇   ?
      ◇ 8 3
      ♣ K 6 2

One spade. When you are changing the suit, there is no need to jump to show your point count, as partner must bid again. On the contrary, you should keep things as low as possible until you know where you are going.

6)   ♠ Q 9 2   **West**   **East**
      ♡ 1 0 7   1◇   ?
      ◇ Q 7 6 4
      ♣ A K 6 3

Three diamonds. With four-card support your first duty is to give partner the good news by raising him. You must also show your strength, three diamonds showing around 10–12 points.

7)   ♠ Q 1 0 7 4   **West**   **East**
      ♡ 8 6   1♡   ?
      ◇ A Q J 4 2
      ♣ 7 3

One spade. A tricky one, as you are strong enough to bid a new suit at the two level if you wish to. The trouble is that if it starts 1♡ – 2◇ – 2♡, you are not strong enough to bid again, so a spade fit may be missed. Remember, opener cannot rebid two spades over two diamonds with a minimum hand, but must repeat his hearts even with 5-4.

8)   ♠ Q 1 0 6 5   **West**   **East**
      ♡ A 3   1♡   ?
      ◇ A K 7 6 5
      ♣ 9 4

Two diamonds. This time you can afford to bid your longest suit first, because if partner does rebid two hearts you are strong enough to follow up with two spades.

9)   ♠ Q1074   **West**   **East**
      ♡ AK952   1♡   2♣
      ◇ A6   ?
      ♣ 73

Two hearts. You have a minimum opening, so cannot afford to bid the spades. Two spades would be a reverse, pushing the bidding up a level, and showing a stronger hand, roughly 16 plus HCPs.

10)   ♠ AQ107   **West**   **East**
      ♡ AK952   1♡   2♣
      ◇ A6   ?
      ♣ 73

Two spades. Now that you have the extra strength, you can afford to reverse. Opposite a two-over-one response (9 plus HCPs) you are quite prepared to go to game, as there must be 26 plus points between the two hands.

11)   ♠ AJ1073   **West**   **East**
      ♡ AQ7   1♠   2♠
      ◇ AQ2   ?
      ♣ 64

Three spades. Partner has promised 6–9 HCPs, plus of course spade support. You have enough to be interested in game but not enough to be sure about it. Three spades invites partner to bid game with a maximum (8–9 HCPs) but pass with a minimum (6–7 HCPs).

12)   ♠ A4   **West**   **East**
      ♡ AQ1085   1♡   1NT
      ◇ AKJ87   ?
      ♣ 10

Three diamonds. With a second five-card suit, you must give partner a choice, and you must also show your great strength by jumping, as game is likely to be on even opposite a mere 6–9 HCPs. The jump in a new suit forces partner to speak again.

13)   ♠ K1073   **West**   **East**
      ♡ AQJ64   1♡   1♠
      ◇ AQ   ?
      ♣ 94

Three spades. You like partner's spades, so must support him. You also have extra strength, so must jump, three spades showing about 16–18 total points.

14)	♠ A Q 4	**West**	**East**
	♡ J 10 7 5	1♡	1♠
	◇ A K 7	?	
	♣ Q 6 3		

1NT. A balanced hand, which was only opened one heart because you were too strong for 1NT. What could be more natural than to rebid 1NT now?

15)	♠ K 3	**West**	**East**
	♡ Q J 6 4	1♡	2♡
	◇ 10 8 6 4	3♡	?
	♣ 9 7 3		

Pass. Partner is inviting game, but you are minimum for your initial response, so must decline.

16)	♠ A K 3	**West**	**East**
	♡ 10 5 4 2	1♡	2♡
	◇ J 10 9 4	3♡	?
	♣ 7 6		

Four hearts. Your hearts may be weak, but overall the hand is a near maximum, so as partner is inviting game *knowing* that you only have 6–9 points you should accept.

17)	♠ 7 4	**West**	**East**
	♡ J 3 2	1♠	1NT
	◇ K J 7 3	2♣	?
	♣ A 7 3 2		

Three clubs. You have genuine club support and, while you could just pass, with a complete maximum it is best to raise, in case partner has a good hand.

18)	♠ J 3	**West**	**East**
	♡ K Q 4 2	1♠	1NT
	◇ 10 7 6 4 3	2♣	?
	♣ J 3		

Two spades. You do not like either of partner's suits, but you have no reason to suppose that either of yours will prove any better, so should just choose between his suits as cheaply as possible. Give preference to spades, as he will normally have more of them.

19) ♠ 7
♡ K63
◇ J1074
♣ AJ1097

	West	East
	1♠	2♣
	2♡	?

Pass. You have a minimum two club bid and partner's two heart rebid did not promise any extra strength, so there should not be a game on. As you prefer hearts to spades, pass.

20) ♠ Q4
♡ J64
◇ KQ4
♣ K10975

	West	East
	1♠	2♣
	2♡	?

2NT. A little extra, so you can afford to invite game. As you have no guarantee of an eight-card fit but have the unbid suit well covered, you should bid 2NT, showing about 11 or 12 points.

21) ♠ KJ3
♡ A4
◇ 762
♣ K9863

	West	East
	1♠	2♣
	2♡	?

Three spades. Again you are in the invitational range, but this time you do know of an eight-card fit, so you should support spades. A delayed jump to three spades shows the same strength as an immediate 1♠ – 3♠, the difference being that the delayed bid shows only three-card trump support.

22) ♠ QJ3
♡ 10
◇ J1097
♣ AJ1097

	West	East
	1♡	2♣
	2♠	?

2NT. Partner has reversed, showing a strong hand, so you must bid again. With a sure diamond stop and no guaranteed eight-card fit, no-trumps is the obvious denomination. 2NT is sufficient, as it suggests your minimum hand.

23) ♠ A4
♡ KJ3
◇ 1063
♣ AJ873

	West	East
	1♡	2♣
	2♠	?

Four hearts. Again your partner has reversed, so has a strong hand. He has also guaranteed five hearts, so you have an eight-card fit and can support him. Jump to game to tell him that you also have some extra strength.

24)	♠ A Q 6 4	West	East
	♡ A K 10 7 3	1♡	2♣
	◇ 8 6	2♠	2NT
	♣ A 4	?	

3NT. You have already shown your five hearts and four spades and, within that context, you are as balanced as you could be, so should simply raise to 3NT, trusting partner to have the other suits covered.

25)	♠ A K 6 5	West	East
	♡ A J 10 9 4	1♡	2♣
	◇ 10	2♠	2NT
	♣ A 8 3	?	

Three clubs. Complete the picture of your distribution. You have already promised five hearts and four spades, now tell partner that you have some support for his clubs, in case the diamond stopper is not solid. He will expect only three clubs, because you did not support them immediately.

26)	♠ J 4	West	East
	♡ A Q 3 2	1NT	2♠
	◇ K 7 6 4	?	
	♣ K 10 3		

Pass. Partner has shown a weak hand with long spades. You are obliged to pass whatever your hand.

27)	♠ A 4	West	East
	♡ K J 5 4	1NT	2NT
	◇ J 9 7	?	
	♣ A J 6 2		

3NT. 2NT invites game in no-trumps. Having shown 12–14 HCPs, you are maximum and so should accept the invitation.

28)	♠ Q J 7 3	West	East
	♡ 6	1♡	1♠
	◇ K 6 4 2	2♡	?
	♣ J 8 3 2		

Pass. You dislike hearts, but are far too weak to bid again. After all, you have no guarantee that anything else will be any better.

29)	♠ A J 3 2		West	North	East	South
	♡ K 9 7		1♢	1♠	Pass	?
	♢ 8					
	♣ Q 10 6 4 3					

Three spades. A limit bid in support of partner's overcall. The shape makes your hand far too good for a simple raise to two spades.

30)	♠ Q 10 7 3		West	North	East	South
	♡ 8 4		1♡	1NT	Pass	?
	♢ K Q 5					
	♣ Q J 8 7					

Two clubs. Opposite partner's 15–17 HCPs, you could just raise to 3NT, but it can do no harm to check for a 4-4 spade fit on the way. Two clubs is Stayman, just as it would have been had partner opened 1NT, and you can always bid 3NT on the next round, if partner does not have spades.

31)	♠ 1 0 5 4		West	North	East	South
	♡ Q 7 6 3		1♣	1♠	?	
	♢ A J 5 2					
	♣ 7 4					

Pass. Without the overcall you would have had to respond, but now there is nothing you can bid. You are not strong enough to bid a new suit at the two level, cannot bid no-trumps without a spade stopper, and cannot support clubs with only two. Don't worry, if partner is strong he will bid again.

32)	♠ K 4		West	North	East	South
	♡ J 7 3 2		1♡	1♠	?	
	♢ Q J 6 3					
	♣ 1 0 9 4					

Two hearts. You have 6–9 points and a balanced hand with a spade stopper, but must not bid 1NT, as you also have four-card support for partner's suit and that must always take precedence.

33)	♠ 8		West	North	East	South
	♡ J 1 0 6 3		1♡	Dble	?	
	♢ K Q J 4					
	♣ 7 4 3 2					

Three hearts. A slight stretch, but you know that if you have a fit so must have your opponents. Make it difficult for them to get together, by bidding as high as you can.

34)   ♠ K 4

    ♡ J 7 3 2

    ◇ Q J 6 3

    ♣ 1 0 9 4

West	North	East	South
1♡	1♠	?	

Two hearts. You have 6–9 points and a balanced hand with a spade stopper, but must not bid 1NT, as you also have four-card support for partner's suit and that must always take precedence.

35)   ♠ 8

    ♡ J 1 0 6 3

    ◇ K Q J 4

    ♣ 7 4 3 2

West	North	East	South
1♡	Dble	?	

Three hearts. A slight stretch, but you know that if you have a fit so must have your opponents. Make it difficult for them to get together, by bidding as high as you can.

PUTTING IT ALL TOGETHER
Revision Quiz Two

In each case, what has West shown by his bidding so far?

1)	West	East		2)	West	East
	1♡	2♣				1NT
	2♠	2NT			2♣	2♡
	3♡				2NT	

3)	West	East		4)	West	East
	1NT	2♣			2NT	3◇
	2♡	2NT			3NT	
	4♠					

5)	West	East		6)	West	East
		2NT				2NT
	3♣	3♡			4NT	
	3NT					

7)	West	East		8)	West	East
		2♠				2♠
	3♠				3◇	

9)	West	East		10)	West	East
	2♡	2NT			2♣	2◇
	3◇				2NT	

11)	West	East		12)	West	East
		2♣				2♣
	2NT				2◇	2♠
					3◇	

13)	West	East		14)	West	East
	2♣	2◇			3♡	
	2NT	3♣				
	3◇					

15)	West	East		16)	West	East
	3NT				4♡	

139

17)	West		East	
	3♥		3♠	
	3NT			

18)	West		East	
			3♦	
	3♠			

19)	West	North	East	South
				1♦
	1♠			

20)	West	North	East	South
				1♥
	Dble			

21)	West	North	East	South
		1♦	Dble	Pass
	2♦			

22)	West	North	East	South
		1♥	Dble	Pass
	2♠			

23)	West	North	East	South
				1♥
	1NT			

24)	West	North	East	South
				1♠
	1NT	Pass	2♣	Pass
	2♥			

25)	West	North	East	South
				1♦
	Dble	Pass	1♥	Pass
	3♥			

26)	West	North	East	South
		1NT	Dble	Pass
	2♦			

27)	West	North	East	South
				3♥
	Dble			

28)	West	North	East	South
				3♥
	4♠			

29)	West	North	East	South
		3♦	Dble	Pass
	3♠			

30)	West	North	East	South
			1♦	1♥
	Dble			

31)	West	North	East	South
		1♦	1♥	Pass
	1NT			

32)	West	North	East	South
			1♥	1♠
	1NT			

33)	West	North	East	South
			1♦	Dble
	1♠			

34)	West	North	East	South
			1♥	Dble
	3♥			

28)
West	North	East	South
			3♡
4♠			

29)
West	North	East	South
	3◇	Dble	Pass
3♠			

30)
West	North	East	South
		1◇	1♡
Dble			

31)
West	North	East	South
	1◇	1♡	Pass
1NT			

32)
West	North	East	South
		1♡	1♠
1NT			

33)
West	North	East	South
		1◇	Dble
1♠			

34)
West	North	East	South
		1♡	Dble
3♡			

35)
West	North	East	South
		1◇	Dble
1NT			

Solutions to Revision Quiz Two

1) | West | East |
    |------|------|
    | 1♡ | 2♣ |
    | 2♠ | 2NT |
    | 3♡ | |

West opened one heart then bid two spades — a reverse — so must have
a strong hand, 16 plus points. A reverse also guarantees that the first suit
is longer than the second, so he must have five hearts and four spades, but
then he bid the hearts again, so must have extra length there. His hand is
four spades, six hearts and 16 plus points.

2) | West | East |
    |------|------|
    | | 1NT |
    | 2♣ | 2♡ |
    | 2NT | |

West bid two clubs, Stayman, and on hearing East's two hearts bid 2NT,
inviting game in no-trumps. He must have a flattish 11–12 HCPs and, as he
used Stayman, must have four spades, since he is clearly not interested in
hearts.

3) | West | East |
    |------|------|
    | 1NT | 2♣ |
    | 2♡ | 2NT |
    | 4♠ | |

For his opening bid, West has a balanced 12–14 HCPs. Two hearts showed
a four-card suit and, when East invited game in no-trumps, he jumped to
four spades, so must also have four spades *and* a maximum.

4) | West | East |
    |------|------|
    | 2NT | 3◇ |
    | 3NT | |

West has a balanced 20–22 points with no interest in diamonds.

5) | West | East |
    |------|------|
    | | 2NT |
    | 3♣ | 3♡ |
    | 3NT | |

For his raise to game, he has about 5–10 HCPs in a fairly balanced hand. However, he used Stayman on the way, so must have a four-card major — which must be spades as he did not support hearts.

6) | West | East |
    |------|------|
    | | 2NT |
    | 4NT | |

As he raised no-trumps he is fairly balanced, but he bid one more than was necessary for game, so is inviting slam and has about 11 or 12 points.

7) | West | East |
    |------|------|
    | | 2♠ |
    | 3♠ | |

West has spade support, positive values (7 plus HCPs), and usually at least one ace. With no ace, he would bid four spades unless he were good enough not to want to dampen partner's enthusiasm for slam.

8) | West | East |
    |------|------|
    | | 2♠ |
    | 3♢ | |

West probably does not like spades, but he has a good five-card or longer diamond suit and positive values, at least 7 HCPs.

9) | West | East |
    |------|------|
    | 2♡ | 2NT |
    | 3♢ | |

Two hearts showed a strong hand with a long strong heart suit, at least eight probable playing tricks. Three diamonds is a second suit of at least four cards.

10) | West | East |
|------|------|
| 2♣ | 2♢ |
| 2NT | |

23–24 HCPs and a balanced hand. The two club opening is completely artificial, merely showing a very powerful hand and having nothing to do with clubs. In this case, the rebid shows a hand too good to open 2NT.

11) | West | East |
|------|------|
| | 2♣ |
| 2NT | |

The 2NT response showed around 7–9 HCPs with no good suit and a fairly balanced hand.

12) | West | East |
|------|------|
| | 2♣ |
| 2♢ | 2♠ |
| 3♢ | |

Two diamonds simply showed a weak hand, less than 7–8 HCPs, and had nothing to do with diamonds. Three diamonds, however, shows a diamond suit, though it need not be that great a suit, as West was obliged to bid something. East's rebid is forcing to game.

13) | West | East |
|------|------|
| 2♣ | 2♢ |
| 2NT | 3♣ |
| 3♢ | |

As we have already seen, two clubs followed by 2NT shows 23–24 HCPs and a balanced hand. Three clubs was Stayman, so three diamonds just denied a four-card major, it did not necessarily promise diamonds.

14) | West | East |
|------|------|
| 3♡ | |

An opening bid of three of a suit shows a seven- or eight-card suit — a reasonable one — but not enough high cards to open at the one level, about five or six playing tricks non-vulnerable, six or seven vulnerable.

15) **West**   **East**
    3NT

This opening shows a completely solid seven- or eight-card minor suit and very little outside.

16) **West**   **East**
    4♡

Four hearts shows a very long heart suit, at least seven cards, and too much playing strength to open three hearts but still low in terms of high-card strength.

17) **West**   **East**
    3♡   3♠
    3NT

Three hearts showed a good long heart suit but not many high cards, while 3NT suggests a dislike for spades, with perhaps just a little something in the unbid suits, e.g.

    ♠ 7
    ♡ K Q 10 9 7 6 3
    ♢ J 6 3
    ♣ K 4

18) **West**   **East**
            3♢
    3♠

A powerful hand with a good long spade suit, sufficient to think of game opposite a weak pre-emptive opening and with the possibility of spades being the correct trump suit, even though partner cannot have much support for any suit other than diamonds.

19) **West**   **North**   **East**   **South**
                                      1♢
    1♠

A one-level overcall shows at least a reasonable five-card suit and 8–15 HCPs.

20)	**West**	**North**	**East**	**South**
				1♡
	Dble			

West has made a take-out double, so will have sufficient strength to have opened the bidding himself, had he had the opportunity to do so. He will usually also have support for every suit other than that opened, in this case hearts.

21)	**West**	**North**	**East**	**South**
		1◇	Dble	Pass
	2◇			

He has enough strength to want to play in game but does not know which game it should be. The bid of the opponent's suit sets up a situation where neither player is allowed to pass until game is reached and allows both to bid their suits, until a suitable fit is found.

22)	**West**	**North**	**East**	**South**
		1♡	Dble	Pass
	2♠			

When responding to a take-out double, it is necessary not only to tell partner what suit you like best but also how strong you are. The jump shows that West has not bid just because he was compelled to but actually has something — about 9–12 points — and spades are his favourite suit.

23)	**West**	**North**	**East**	**South**
				1♡
	1NT			

A 1NT overcall shows a fairly balanced hand with 15–17 HCPs and at least one stopper in the opponents' suit.

24)	**West**	**North**	**East**	**South**
				1♠
	1NT	Pass	2♣	Pass
	2♡			

1NT showed 15–17 HCPs and a spade stopper in a balanced hand. Two hearts simply showed four hearts in response to Stayman.

25)	**West**	**North**	**East**	**South**
				1◇
	Dble	Pass	1♡	Pass
	3♡			

West has a very strong hand, expecting to make three hearts opposite virtually nothing more than a four-card heart suit. Remember, East had to respond to the double, so may be very weak indeed. West's three hearts is a strong invitation to game, East being expected to bid on with anything that looks as though it might be useful — 4–5 points, say.

26)	**West**	**North**	**East**	**South**
	—	1NT	Dble	Pass
	2◇			

East's double was for penalties, showing a stronger hand than the opener's. Two diamonds shows a weak hand which cannot stand the double, usually with at least five diamonds.

27)	**West**	**North**	**East**	**South**
				3♡
	Dble			

This is for take-out, just as it would have been over one heart, and shows a good opening hand with support for all the other suits, apart from hearts.

28)	**West**	**North**	**East**	**South**
				3♡
	4♠			

A powerful hand with a long strong spade suit. West is so strong that he does not feel able to bid only three spades, as he needs so little help from partner to be able to make game.

29)	**West**	**North**	**East**	**South**
		3◇	Dble	Pass
	3♠			

In response to a take-out double, a simple bid of a suit shows that the suit, in this case spades, is the longest one in responder's hand and that he is weak — less than about 7–8 HCPs and possibly nothing at all.

30)	**West**	**North**	**East**	**South**
			1♢	1♡
	Dble			

West has a reasonable hand with strong hearts. As the double was not his side's first positive contribution to the auction, it is not for take-out but for penalties. East is expected to pass it out most of the time.

31)	**West**	**North**	**East**	**South**
		1♢	1♡	Pass
	1NT			

About 9–11 HCPs, no great heart support, but a fairly balanced hand with a solid diamond stopper. Note that this bid requires more high cards than if partner had opened the bidding. A one-level overcall could be made on as few as 8–9 points.

32)	**West**	**North**	**East**	**South**
			1♡	1♠
	1NT			

6–9 HCPs and a balanced hand with a stopper in spades and less than four hearts.

33)	**West**	**North**	**East**	**South**
			1♢	Dble
	1♠			

West has 6 plus points and a spade suit. If the spades are only four cards in length they should be strong, as there is little point in mentioning a weak four-card suit when an opponent has already shown interest in that suit by making a take-out double.

34)	**West**	**North**	**East**	**South**
			1♡	Dble
	3♡			

At least four-card support and in principle about 10–12 points just as without the double, however West may be stretching a little to make life difficult for his opponents, who must also have a fit somewhere.

35) | West | East | North | South |
|---|---|---|---|
| — | — | 1◇ | Dble |
| 1NT | | | |

The 1NT response is not really affected by the intervening double, except that it may now include a weak four-card major. Basically, however, it still shows a balanced 6–9 points with less than four diamonds.

SECTION FOUR
SOME MORE ADVANCED IDEAS

The game try

When the auction begins 1♠ – 2♠ or 1♡ – 2♡, the opener knows that his partner has four-card support for his suit and also that he has around 6–9 total points. Often, this will be sufficient information for him to decide immediately either that game is on or that there is definitely not enough between the two hands for game. When opener holds around 17–18 points he will be unsure whether or not to bid game, so will want to make an invitational bid and leave it up to partner to decide.

So far we have kept things fairly simple, suggesting that the way to invite game is to re-raise the agreed trump suit to the three level, i.e. 1♡ – 2♡ – 3♡ or 1♠ – 2♠ – 3♠. Responder then bids game with a maximum but passes with a minimum. That is fair enough, and is sufficiently accurate, and quite complicated enough, for the needs of the beginner. As you gain in experience, however, you discover that it is not only the number of high cards which the partnership holds but also how well they fit together which decides the success or failure of a contract. Look at these two examples:

a) ♠xxx opposite ♠xxx
   ♣Axx opposite ♣Kxx

b) ♠xxx opposite ♠Kxx
   ♣Axx opposite ♣xxx

In position a) you can be certain of two tricks with the ace-king; in position b) you can still be sure of making the ace of clubs but the king of spades is only a 50% proposition depending on which opponent has the ace, so you have only one and a half tricks instead of two, despite having the same values as before.

c) ♠KJx opposite ♠Qxx
   ♣xxx opposite ♣x

d) ♠KJx opposite ♠x
   ♣xxx opposite ♣Qxx

Assuming that you have an adequate trump fit elsewhere, there are just two losers in c), one in each suit, while the same high cards fit together much less well in d), so that there are three, or more likely four, losers because the king-jack are wasted opposite the other hand's shortage.

Usually, where the two partners have already bid other suits before finding a fit, they have some idea of where the other hand's strength is likely to be. When a suit is agreed upon immediately this is not the case, however, the very fact that a suit has been agreed means that it is perfectly safe to bid a second suit to help partner to judge how high to go, without there being any danger of ending up in the wrong suit. For example, after 1♠ – 2♠, bid three diamonds with:

♠ A J 10 6 3
♡ A K J
♢ Q 10 7 3
♣ 6

but three clubs with:

♠ A J 10 6 3
♡ A K J
♢ 6
♣ Q 10 7 3

Partner knows that spades are going to be trumps, but hearing about your second suit will help him to judge whether or not his high cards are fitting well. It is better for them to be in your long suits than in your short suits, where they may be wasted. If he has a close decision whether or not to bid game, this will help him to guess right far more often than if you just showed your 18 points (15 HCPs + 3 for the singleton), by raising to three spades. Say responder holds:

♠ K 9 7 4
♡ 6 5
♢ K J 4
♣ 9 8 5 2

He will be very encouraged to hear you bid three diamonds — where he has the king and jack — but discouraged by three clubs where he has nothing.

If opener does not have a second suit to show he can still simply re-raise the agreed trump suit as before if he has a long suit, or bid 2NT with a fairly balanced hand. Now responder knows to look at his high cards in every suit to decide how high to go.

QUIZ THIRTEEN
The game try

What is your next bid?

1) ♠ A Q 10 7 3
    ♡ A J 4 2
    ♢ Q 3
    ♣ 7 6

	West	East
	1♠	2♠
	?	

2) ♠ A Q 10 7 3
    ♡ A K
    ♢ K 10 7 4
    ♣ 7 2

	West	East
	1♠	2♠
	?	

3) ♠ A Q J 7 4 2
    ♡ 10 6
    ♢ K 3
    ♣ A Q 2

	West	East
	1♠	2♠
	?	

4) ♠ A Q 7 4
    ♡ A K 3
    ♢ K 6 2
    ♣ Q 10 4

	West	East
	1♠	2♠
	?	

5) ♠ A Q J 7 4
    ♡ A K 3
    ♢ A J 10
    ♣ 7 2

	West	East
	1♠	2♠
	?	

6) ♠ A 6
    ♡ Q J 7 4
    ♢ 10 8 3
    ♣ Q 10 6 4

	West	East
	1♡	2♡
	3♢	?

7) ♠ J 3 2
    ♡ Q J 10 3
    ♢ K 3
    ♣ 7 6 4 2

	West	East
	1♡	2♡
	3♢	?

152

8) ♠ Q J 2   West   East
    ♡ Q J 8 4   1♡   2♡
    ◇ 7 6 2   3◇   ?
    ♣ Q 9 3

9) ♠ A 4 2   West   East
    ♡ K 1 0 6 3   1♡   2♡
    ◇ J 4   2NT   ?
    ♣ 1 0 8 6 2

10) ♠ 8 6 3 2   West   East
    ♡ Q 7 6 2   1♡   2♡
    ◇ J 6 4   2NT   ?
    ♣ K 7

11) ♠ Q 6 2   West   East
    ♡ K Q 4 3   1♡   2♡
    ◇ J 7 2   3♡   ?
    ♣ 1 0 4 2

12) ♠ K 7   West   East
    ♡ 1 0 8 6 2   1♡   2♡
    ◇ A 6 3   3♡   ?
    ♣ 9 6 4 2

SOLUTIONS TO QUIZ THIRTEEN
The game try

1)	♠ A Q 10 7 3		West	East
	♡ A J 4 2		1♠	2♠
	◇ Q 3		?	
	♣ 7 6			

Pass. Opposite 6–9 points, there cannot be enough strength between the two hands for game.

2)	♠ A Q 10 7 3		West	East
	♡ A K		1♠	2♠
	◇ K 10 7 4		?	
	♣ 7 2			

Three diamonds. 16 HCPs plus two doubletons make this hand worth a game try. Bid the second suit and partner will look particularly favourably on high cards in diamonds.

3)	♠ A Q J 7 4 2		West	East
	♡ 10 6		1♠	2♠
	◇ K 3		?	
	♣ A Q 2			

Three spades. Again you are worth a try for game, but this time you should tell partner that you have extra length in spades and no second suit.

4)	♠ A Q 7 4		West	East
	♡ A K 3		1♠	2♠
	◇ K 6 2		?	
	♣ Q 10 4			

2NT. 18 HCPs, so you must invite game. Let partner know that you are very flat, by bidding no-trumps, now he will know that *all* his high cards are important.

5) ♠ A Q J 7 4
   ♡ A K 3
   ◇ A J 10
   ♣ 7 2

West	East
1♠	2♠
?	

Four spades. 19 HCPs plus a five-card suit — plenty for game, so bid it immediately.

6) ♠ A 6
   ♡ Q J 7 4
   ◇ 1 0 8 3
   ♣ Q 10 6 4

West	East
1♡	2♡
3◇	?

Four hearts. A poor diamond holding, but absolutely maximum, so you should accept *any* invitational bid.

7) ♠ J 3 2
   ♡ Q J 10 3
   ◇ K 3
   ♣ 7 6 4 2

West	East
1♡	2♡
3◇	?

Four hearts. Near minimum in high cards, but an excellent diamond holding, as you have help both in the form of a high card and in the ability to ruff later.

8) ♠ Q J 2
   ♡ Q J 8 4
   ◇ 7 6 2
   ♣ Q 9 3

West	East
1♡	2♡
3◇	?

Three hearts. 8 HCPs, but no help in diamonds and some of your points in the black suits may be wasted, as partner must be short in one of them.

9) ♠ A 4 2
   ♡ K 10 6 3
   ◇ J 4
   ♣ 1 0 8 6 2

West	East
1♡	2♡
2NT	?

Four hearts. Partner is balanced, but you are sufficiently near maximum to accept his invitation.

10)	♠ 8632		**West**	**East**
	♡ Q762		1♡	2♡
	◇ J64		2NT	?
	♣ K7			

Three hearts. This time you are weak, so should decline any game invitation. Remember, however, to return to the agreed trump suit, rather than just pass.

11)	♠ Q62		**West**	**East**
	♡ KQ43		1♡	2♡
	◇ J72		3♡	?
	♣ 1042			

Pass. A tricky one, but if partner is very long in hearts, then your queen is no more use than would be a small card. The ace and king will be sufficient to draw all the opposing trumps. What little you have outside may be useless, as partner must be short in one or two of the other suits.

12)	♠ K7		**West**	**East**
	♡ 10862		1♡	2♡
	◇ A63		3♡	?
	♣ 9642			

Four hearts. Even opposite a two- or three-card suit an ace or a king will always prove useful, so here your high cards are all working well and you should bid the game, even though you actually have a point less than in the previous example.

Fourth suit forcing

The basic idea behind fourth suit forcing is both simple and logical. If you and your partner have already bid three suits, it is most unlikely that you will have an eight-card fit in the fourth suit, and so, unlikely that you will have any real wish or need to bid the fourth suit in a natural sense. If you do have a good holding in the fourth suit, you will usually be able to make a limit bid in no-trumps, whilst with a hand too weak for this, you can choose between partner's two suits. This releases a bid of the fourth suit for use as a conventional bid, saying nothing about your holding in the suit but asking partner to describe his hand further. For example, if you did not have fourth suit forcing available, a bidding problem like the following would be insoluble. You hold something like:

♠ A 10 7 4 2
♡ A 6
♢ 10 8 4
♣ K Q 3

and the bidding goes one heart from partner, one spade from you, two clubs from partner; what do you do? With your 13 HCPs opposite an opening bid you clearly want to play in game, but can only guess which — four hearts, four spades, five clubs or 3NT, could all be right, depending on partner's hand, while even six clubs or six spades could be on with 3NT losing the first five tricks. Fourth suit forcing saves you the guess. You just bid two diamonds and let partner make a further descriptive bid. After you have heard his response you should be much better placed to pick the correct final contract. If partner bids 2NT you can raise, confident that he has a diamond stopper, while if he bids clubs, spades or hearts, that suit should be trumps, as he must have something extra in whichever suit he chooses — something which he had not previously promised.

Fourth suit forcing is tremendously useful when it occurs, but also, suitable hands for its use come up far more frequently than ones on which you might want to make the same bid naturally. In fact, it is only with a weak misfitting two-suiter that you lose anything at all, e.g. after 1♡ – 1♠ – 2♣ – ?, it would be nice if you could bid two diamonds, natural and non-forcing, with:

♠ Q 10 8 6 4
♡ 7 4
♢ K J 6 3 2
♣ J

157

but even then there is a tolerable, albeit slightly unappetising, alternative, namely giving preference to two hearts. With a strong two-suited hand, nothing is lost, as you can still show your second suit by bidding and then rebidding it on the next round, if it seems appropriate to do so. For example, 1♡ – 1♠ – 2♣ – 2◇ – any – 3◇ with:

♠ A Q J 7 3 2
♡ 8
◇ A Q J 6 4
♣ 9

I am not suggesting that fourth suit is an alternative to making a natural bid. If there is a natural bid available which will describe the strength and shape of your hand, you should make it. The fourth suit is only used when you do not have a satisfactory natural bid available, so would prefer a non-committal bid for the time being. Partner is expected to show the most significant feature of his hand that you do not yet know about — and as well as showing the shape of his hand, he should show any significant extra strength by jumping. To be sure of always being able to cope with any rebid partner might make, even in a suit which does not appeal to you, you should have upwards of 10 points to use the fourth suit bid — in other words, the strength to go to the level of 2NT, but a hand where that bid is inappropriate, probably because you do not have the unbid suit adequately covered. This is an area of bidding which can become quite complex, and it is not within the scope of this book to go into all of its complexities. Even in its simplest form fourth suit forcing is an invaluable aid to accurate bidding. A few examples will test your understanding of the basic idea and also explain in a little more detail just what happens after a bid of the fourth suit.

QUIZ FOURTEEN
Fourth suit forcing

What is your next bid?

			West	East
1)	♠ 1095		West	East
	♡ K85		1♣	1◇
	◇ AJ1074		1♡	?
	♣ K6			

			West	East
2)	♠ AQ75		West	East
	♡ Q6		1♡	1♠
	◇ K1097		2♣	?
	♣ 1043			

			West	East
3)	♠ AQ742		West	East
	♡ 9		1♣	1◇
	◇ KQ10976		1♡	?
	♣ 5			

			West	East
4)	♠ Q1076		West	East
	♡ AJ84		1♣	1◇
	◇ 10		1♡	1♠
	♣ AJ103		?	

			West	East
5)	♠ 64		West	East
	♡ AQ32		1♣	1◇
	◇ 7		1♡	1♠
	♣ AQ8742		?	

			West	East
6)	♠ AQ4		West	East
	♡ KJ1072		1♡	2♣
	◇ AQ63		2◇	2♠
	♣ 7		?	

			West	East
7)	♠ K4		West	East
	♡ QJ987		1♣	1◇
	◇ None		1♡	1♠
	♣ KQ10964		?	

8) ♠ Q4
    ♡ KJ873
    ◇ 6
    ♣ AQ1064

West	East
1♡	1♠
2♣	2◇
?	

9) ♠ 863
    ♡ AQ973
    ◇ 10
    ♣ AK74

West	East
1♡	1♠
2♣	2◇
?	

SOLUTIONS TO QUIZ FOURTEEN
Fourth suit forcing

1) ♠ 1095   West   East
   ♡ K85   1♣   1◇
   ◇ AJ1074   1♡   ?
   ♣ K6

One spade. You cannot support either of partner's suits and the diamonds are not worth repeating. 2NT would show the strength and shape of the hand, but unfortunately you don't have a spade stopper. This is an ideal hand for an artificial fourth suit bid to ask partner for further information.

2) ♠ AQ75   West   East
   ♡ Q6   1♡   1♠
   ◇ K1097   2♣   ?
   ♣ 1043

2NT. When you have a good holding in the unbid suit there is rarely any point in bidding it — particularly when it is a minor suit. 2NT shows your hand well, about 11 or 12 points, no fit, but the unbid suit well held.

3) ♠ AQ742   West   East
   ♡ 9   1♣   1◇
   ◇ KQ10976   1♡   ?
   ♣ 5

One spade. When you are strong enough, as here, to bid the fourth suit and then repeat it, you should do so to show your genuine two-suiter. Even three-card support would make spades the right trump suit, so the possibility should be explored. With a weak two-suiter you could not afford to do this, as you might get too high when there proved to be no fit.

4) ♠ Q1076   West   East
   ♡ AJ84   1♣   1◇
   ◇ 10   1♡   1♠
   ♣ AJ103   ?

Two spades. What is the most significant feature of this hand which partner does not yet know of? Your spade suit, of course. Just in case partner has four spades, you should support them. If he doesn't like spades he can always convert to no-trumps, knowing that you have them covered.

161

5)	♠ 64		**West**	**East**
	♡ A Q 3 2		1♣	1♢
	♢ 7		1♡	1♠
	♣ A Q 8 7 4 2		?	

Two clubs. The only unknown feature of this hand is the extra club length.

6)	♠ A Q 4		**West**	**East**
	♡ K J 10 7 2		1♡	2♣
	♢ A Q 6 3		2♢	2♠
	♣ 7		?	

3NT. You have the fourth suit well covered and must jump to show your extra values, as if you only bid 2NT partner, with a bare 11 HCPs, may pass and game be missed.

7)	♠ K 4		**West**	**East**
	♡ Q J 9 8 7		1♣	1♢
	♢ None		1♡	1♠
	♣ K Q 10 9 6 4		?	

Two hearts. True, you have a spade stopper, but 1NT hardly describes this hand properly. With such extreme distribution you should stress that this is a hand to play in one of your suits. Two hearts shows the fifth heart but also the sixth club, because with 5-5 you would have bid hearts first, so the clubs must be longer.

8)	♠ Q 4		**West**	**East**
	♡ K J 8 7 3		1♡	1♠
	♢ 6		2♣	2♢
	♣ A Q 10 6 4		?	

Three clubs. So far you have shown 5-4, now show the fifth club by rebidding them.

9)	♠ 863		**West**	**East**
	♡ A Q 9 7 3		1♡	1♠
	♢ 10		2♣	2♢
	♣ A K 7 4		?	

Two spades. You have already denied four spades, as you did not raise them immediately, so the main new feature to show is that you have secondary spade support.

9)   ♠ Q 4

     ♡ K J 8 7 3

     ♢ 6

     ♣ A Q 10 6 4

West	East
1♡	1♠
2♣	2♢
?	

Three clubs. So far you have shown 5-4, now show the fifth club by rebidding them.

10)   ♠ 8 6 3

     ♡ A Q 9 7 3

     ♢ 10

     ♣ A K 7 4

West	East
1♡	1♠
2♣	2♢
?	

Two spades. You have already denied four spades, as you did not raise them immediately, so the main new feature to show is that you have secondary spade support.

The jump shift response

So far we have said that responder should only jump the bidding when he knows where he is going. In other words, when he is making a limit bid in support of partner's suit or in no-trumps and wants to show the strength of his hand. When bidding a new suit we have seen that there is no need to jump, because even a simple change of suit is forcing on partner who must find another bid.

If you never did jump in a new suit, you probably would not encounter too many problems, nonetheless there are occasional hands which are best expressed by starting with a jump — called a jump shift. These are very strong hands with a good suit, where if you did not jump at your first opportunity you might have an awkward bid on the next round.

A bid such as 1♡ – 2♠ or 1♠ – 3♣ then, shows about 16 plus HCPs and a strong suit. It is a hand on which game is a certainty opposite an opening bid and slam a distinct possibility. Clearly then, a jump shift has to be forcing. Neither partner may pass until at least a game contract has been reached, so having jumped once there is no need to do so again, just to make sure that partner keeps bidding.

Let's look at a few examples:

			West	East
1)	♠	AKJ1073	West	East
	♡	A4	1♡	?
	◇	KQ3		
	♣	76		

With 17 HCPs and a powerful six-card suit you should immediately consider the possibility that this could be a slam hand. It is also an ideal hand for a jump shift. After 1♡ – 2♠ you can rebid three spades to stress the suit whatever partner's rebid may be. If, on the other hand, you started with one spade and partner rebid two hearts, say, you would have an awkward problem, as you would want to bid spades again but neither two spades nor three spades would be forcing, so you would have to guess what to do.

			West	East
2)	♠	AQ74	West	East
	♡	K63	1♡	?
	◇	AJ102		
	♣	K7		

One spade. This time there is no need to jump even with 17 HCPs. When you are so balanced there will only be a slam if partner has extra values and the best way to find out whether or not he has is to keep the bidding low and hear his natural rebid. The other point is that you do not particularly wish to stress the spades to the exclusion of everything else but need to leave as much room as possible to explore which is the best trump suit.

3)	♠ 1063	West	East
	♡ Q63	1♡	?
	◇ A K J 10 9		
	♣ A K		

Three diamonds. Again, you have a powerful suit in a strong hand. Get the strength off your chest immediately with a jump shift and partner will be well placed to cooperate in the search for a slam if there is one. A simple two diamond response might leave you in difficulties with your rebid.

4)	♠ Q64	West	East
	♡ KQ1073	1♡	2♠
	◇ AK	?	
	♣ 1063		

Three spades. Over a one spade response you would have rebid the hearts, but now that partner has promised a powerful suit ♠Qxx should be ample support.

5)	♠ 72	West	East
	♡ KQ1063	1♡	2♠
	◇ AJ4	?	
	♣ AJ7		

2NT. You could rebid the hearts, but basically this is a balanced hand with the only weakness being in partner's suit. If partner has three hearts, he can always bid them over 2NT.

6)	♠ 7	West	East
	♡ AQ1052	1♡	2♠
	◇ K63	?	
	♣ KJ108		

Three clubs. Where you have a second suit, you bid it, just as you would have done a level lower, had partner not jumped.

7) ♠ A K J 10 7 3   West   East
    ♡ A 4   1♡   2♠
    ◇ 7 6   3♣   ?
    ♣ K Q 3

Three spades. This is why you jumped to two spades, so that you could stress the spades, by bidding them again without any fear of partner passing you out short of game.

8) ♠ A K J 10 7   West   East
    ♡ K 6 3   1♡   2♠
    ◇ A 4   3♣   ?
    ♣ Q 7 2

Three hearts. You have already shown a strong spade suit, so the major feature of your hand which partner does not yet know about is the quite respectable secondary heart support. As partner has virtually guaranteed five hearts by rebidding in a second suit, it is quite likely that they should be the trump suit, despite your five spades.

9) ♠ 10 3   West   East
    ♡ A Q 10 5 2   1♡   2♠
    ◇ J 6   3♣   3♠
    ♣ A Q J 4   ?

Four spades. You have already shown both your suits and, now that partner has jumped in and rebid spades, he must have a very good suit, so 10-x is ample support.

10) ♠ 7   West   East
    ♡ K J 10 7 3   1♡   2♠
    ◇ K J 4   3♣   3♠
    ♣ A J 7 4   ?

3NT. This time you are not happy about spades but have a strong holding in the unbid suit, so a no-trump bid will nicely complete a picture of your hand and should be the right contract, unless partner bids again.

Slam bidding

Bidding slams can be dangerous as, if you misjudge and get too high, you lose not only the penalty points for going down in your contract, but also the points you would have scored had you settled for game. On the other hand, bidding and making a slam is both exciting and profitable — you will score roughly twice as much for making a slam as for making the same twelve tricks but only bidding game.

The easiest slams to bid are those which are reached on sheer power, where just adding HCPs together tells you that there should be a good chance of making twelve tricks. For example:

♠ A Q 7
♡ K J 3
♢ Q 6 4 2
♣ Q 10 2

opposite a 2NT opening — there must be 34–36 HCPs between the two hands so you should bid 6NT. If there are no long suits, then around 33 points will be needed to make slam a good bet.

If there is an adequate trump fit, merely counting points will not be sufficient. In unbalanced hands, long suits may provide extra tricks, as indeed may shortages. Judgement of how well the two hands fit together is essential, but also needed are ways to check that there are not two or more quick losers, which could prove fatal even if twelve tricks would otherwise be available. Obviously it is no use to have sixteen winners, if you have lost the first two tricks.

There are two approaches which can be tried to check that you have the necessary control cards for a slam. Neither should be used until you know what suit is going to be trumps — that must always be settled first.

a) THE BLACKWOOD CONVENTION

The Blackwood convention is a way of asking partner how many aces he holds, via an artificial bid of 4NT. Obviously this pushes the bidding to the five level, so it can only be used when you already know that there is a great deal of strength between the two hands. Rather than being a way of bidding slams, it is really a way of staying out of bad ones, and should only be used when you are pretty confident that there should be twelve tricks, as long as you do not have two aces missing. It is also of course essential if you are thinking of bidding a grand slam, where you must have first-round control of every suit.

For example, you open two clubs on:

♠ K Q 3
♡ K Q J 4
◇ A K Q J 2
♣ A

and partner makes a positive response of two hearts. With an excellent fit for hearts and a very powerful hand, your thoughts immediately turn to slam. Basically, there are only two cards you are interested in — the two missing aces — and if you knew whether partner held them, you would be very well placed to decide on the final contract. This is an ideal hand for Blackwood. If partner has no ace, you will have to settle for five hearts; if he has one, there should be a small slam; while if he has both, there should be no loser, so you can bid seven.

The responses to a Blackwood 4NT are as follows:

5♣	=	0 or 4 aces
5◇	=	1 ace
5♡	=	2 aces
5♠	=	3 aces

There should never be any ambiguity over the five club response. If you cannot tell whether partner has 0 or 4 aces, what on earth are you doing looking for a slam in the first place?

Once the 4NT bidder knows his partner's aces, he can follow up with a 5NT bid to ask for kings. Again the responses follow a step principle.

6♣	=	0 kings
6◇	=	1 king
6♡	=	2 kings
6♠	=	3 kings
6NT	=	4 kings

Generally, you should only ask for kings if you know that the partnership holds all the aces and you are interested in a grand slam. 5NT commits you to the six level and, if an ace is missing, you can never go higher. The number of kings partner holds will not make any difference to your final decision — will it?

One final reminder, you must know what trumps are going to be *before* you use 4NT, as you will not be able to find out later. You should also be fairly sure that there will be twelve tricks, if partner gives a satisfactory response.

b) CUE-BIDDING

Not all potential slam hands are suitable for Blackwood, indeed probably the majority are not. Its attraction is its simplicity, but because it only tells you *how many* aces partner holds and not *which* it is not always a very accurate tool. Fortunately, there is another way in which you can find out which control cards partner has — cue-bidding.

In simple terms, once you have agreed on one suit as trumps, there is no need to look any further. We have already seen the game try, e.g. 1♠ – 2♠ – 3♣, where you bid a second suit to help partner to judge whether or not to go on to game. Once you are already committed to game, a new suit bid cannot mean that and so can be used in a different way. For example, 1♠ – 3♠ – 4♣, says "partner, I am pleased to hear that you like my suit. I am strong enough to be interested in slam and I have first- round control of clubs (ace or void), e.g.

> ♠ A Q 10 9 7
> ♡ A K Q 4
> ◇ 7 3
> ♣ A 5

If you think your hand might be suitable, perhaps you might show me where you have a control as well, by bidding the suit."

It is also permissible to cue-bid a second-round control (king or singleton), but generally only when you have no more first round controls to show. Usually, both players bid their cheapest control first, e.g. after 1♠ – 3♠, with the aces of both clubs and diamonds, you would bid four clubs, the lower one, first. Indeed, a four diamond cue-bid would tend to deny first round control of clubs.

Cue-bidding is much more difficult to use than Blackwood. The first time you try it out you may get into a muddle — most of us did — but used properly, it is a valuable and extremely accurate aid to slam bidding. Remember though, it is no good having all the aces and kings if you have nothing to back them up. Don't go looking for a slam unless you think you can see where the twelve tricks might come from, if you do find that you have all the necessary controls.

c) GRAND SLAM FORCE (GSF)

The one suit which cannot be cue-bid is, of course, the agreed trump suit. A return to that suit by either player is a sign off, saying that he cannot go any further on his own and cannot cue-bid anything else. This means that it is sometimes difficult to be sure that there isn't a hole in the trump suit. That may be acceptable for a small slam, where a trick can be lost, but for a grand slam the trump suit must be completely solid.

The "grand slam force" allows you to ask partner how good his trumps are. After a trump suit has been agreed, a bid of 5NT, when *not* preceded by 4NT (Blackwood), asks how many of the top three trump honours partner holds. There are different versions of the convention, but the following is as good as any. The responses to 5NT vary, depending on which suit is trumps.

When hearts or spades are trumps:

6♣	=	0 top honour
6◇	=	1 top honour
6♡	=	2 top honours
7 of the agreed trumps	=	3 top honours

When diamonds are trumps:

6♣	=	0 top honours
6◇	=	1 top honour
7◇	=	2 top honours

When clubs are trumps:

6♣	=	0 or 1 top honour
7♣	=	2 or 3 top honours

So, when hearts or spades are trumps, it is possible to discover exactly how many top honours partner has. There is not enough room to be exact, when clubs or diamonds have been agreed. When a minor suit is trumps, it is dangerous to use GSF, unless you have at least one top honour yourself. Partner will bid seven with two or three, and if you do not have one yourself, there could be one missing — fatal for a grand slam.

The other important thing to remember is that, just as with Blackwood, you should only use GSF if the answer will solve your problem and tell you how high to go. That means that you must be able to see twelve tricks, even if partner gives an unsatisfactory response and thirteen tricks, if you do have all the top trumps. This is vital as, having asked the question about trumps, there will be no room to explore any further. You will have to make your final decision next.

QUIZ FIFTEEN
Slam bidding

What is your next bid?

1) ♠ K Q J 10 4
    ♡ K Q J 9 7
    ◇ 6
    ♣ K Q

West	East
1♠	?

2) ♠ K Q J 9 4 2
    ♡ A K
    ◇ 7
    ♣ K Q 10 4

West	East
1◇	2♠
3♠	?

3) ♠ K 3
    ♡ K Q 9 7 4 2
    ◇ 10 6
    ♣ A Q 4

West	East
1♠	2♡
4♡	?

4) ♠ A 9 3
    ♡ A 10 8
    ◇ K J 7
    ♣ Q 10 7 4

West	East
1◇	3NT
4♣	?

5) ♠ A K Q 10 4
    ♡ A 3
    ◇ Q J 9 5 2
    ♣ 6

West	East
1♣	1♠
2◇	?

6) ♠ A 5 4
    ♡ K Q J 7 2
    ◇ K 3
    ♣ A J 4

West	East
1♣	2♡
3♡	?

7) ♠ A 3 2
    ♡ Q 10 7 4
    ◇ A J 6 4
    ♣ 9 6

West	East
1♡	3♡
4♣	?

8)   ♠ KQJ
    ♡ KQJ87
    ◇ AQ86
    ♣ 7

West	East
1♡	3♡
4◇	4♠
?	

9)   ♠ KQ
    ♡ 10632
    ◇ K874
    ♣ Q32

West	East
1♡	3♡
4♣	?

10) ♠ 8764
    ♡ K764
    ◇ AQ3
    ♣ 72

West	East
2♡	3♡
3♠	4◇
5NT	?

SOLUTIONS TO QUIZ FIFTEEN
Slam bidding

1)	♠ K Q J 10 4		West	East
	♡ K Q J 9 7		1♠	?
	♢ 6			
	♣ K Q			

4NT. An ideal hand for Blackwood with excellent trumps, a source of tricks outside, and second-round control of every suit. The only thing that matters is how many aces partner has — if four, there will be thirteen tricks; if three, twelve; if two then only eleven. He is most unlikely to only have one ace, when you have so many of the other high cards.

2)	♠ K Q J 9 4 2		West	East
	♡ A K		1♢	2♠
	♢ 7		3♣	?
	♣ K Q 10 4			

4NT. You have at least second-round control of every suit and no real losers apart from the aces. Once again, Blackwood should tell you how high to go. Bid seven spades opposite three, six spades opposite two, and otherwise five spades.

3)	♠ K 3		West	East
	♡ K Q 9 7 4 2		1♠	2♡
	♢ 10 6		4♡	?
	♣ A Q 4			

Five clubs. Having heard that partner not only likes hearts but is also strong — he jumped — you can expect to make a slam as long as there are not two quick losers. This time Blackwood won't necessarily help since, if partner shows two aces, there could be two top losers — e.g.

> ♠ A Q J 10 7
> ♡ A J 10 3
> ♢ 7 4
> ♣ K 6

or slam could be cold —

> ♠ Q J 10 7 4
> ♡ A J 10 3
> ♢ A
> ♣ K 6 3

You need to make sure that there are not two diamond losers, and the way to do so is to cue-bid clubs, showing a club control and slam interest. Partner may be able to bid slam himself or alternatively cue-bid five diamonds in turn. If he can only bid five hearts, you must pass, as he will be denying a diamond control.

4)	♠ A 9 3		**West**	**East**
	♡ A 10 8		1◇	3NT
	◇ K J 7		4♣	?
	♣ Q 10 7 4			

Four hearts. A new concept. You cannot have four hearts, as you would have bid one heart over one diamond. Four hearts is an advance cue-bid, showing the ace of hearts and a hand suitable for slam in partner's last bid suit — clubs. If partner has a suitable hand, this may encourage him to bid the slam. Look at how good your hand is — useful cards in both partner's suits and aces in his short suits — absolutely nothing wasted.

5)	♠ A K Q 10 4		**West**	**East**
	♡ A 3		1♣	1♠
	◇ Q J 9 5 2		2◇	?
	♣ 6			

4NT. Two diamonds was a reverse, showing a strong hand. With your powerful spades and great trump support, you should immediately think of slam. All that matters is, are there two top losers? — a problem which Blackwood should resolve.

6)	♠ A 5 4		**West**	**East**
	♡ K Q J 7 2		1♣	2♡
	◇ K 3		3♡	?
	♣ A J 4			

Three spades. Blackwood will not solve this one. Though you have a control in every suit, you cannot be sure of twelve tricks. Tell partner you are interested in slam by showing your cheapest control. You will have a better idea of how high to go, when you have heard whether or not partner can cooperate in a slam hunt.

7)	♠ A 3 2		**West**	**East**
	♡ Q 10 7 4		1♡	3♡
	◇ A J 6 4		4♣	?
	♣ 9 6			

Four diamonds. Partner's four clubs was a cue-bid, showing club control and slam interest. You have a perfectly acceptable three heart bid. Cooperate by showing your cheapest control in turn.

8)　♠ KQJ　　　　　　　　　　West　　East
　　♡ KQJ87　　　　　　　　　1♡　　3♡
　　◇ AQ86　　　　　　　　　 4◇　　4♠
　　♣ 7　　　　　　　　　　　 ?

Five clubs. Partner's four heart cue-bid was good news but, as well as two aces, you need him to have the king of diamonds if slam is to be a good bet. Cue-bid again and see if he can show that card by bidding five diamonds, or perhaps he can bid the slam himself.

9)　♠ KQ　　　　　　　　　　 West　　East
　　♡ 10632　　　　　　　　　1♡　　3♡
　　◇ K874　　　　　　　　　 4♣　　?
　　♣ Q32

Four hearts. You have no ace and generally a very poor hand for your previous bidding. You should make the weakest bid you can — sign off in four hearts.

10)　♠ 8764　　　　　　　　　 West　　East
　　 ♡ K764　　　　　　　　　2♡　　3♡
　　 ◇ AQ3　　　　　　　　　 3♠　　4◇
　　 ♣ 72　　　　　　　　　　5NT　　?

Six diamonds. 5NT asked how many of the top three trumps you held. With one the answer is six diamonds. The rest of your hand is irrelevant, you have been asked a specific question so you must answer.

11)	♠ 8 7 6 4		**West**	**East**
	♡ K 7 6 4		2♡	3♡
	◇ A Q 3		3♠	4◇
	♣ 7 2		5NT	?

Six diamonds. 5NT asked how many of the top three trumps you held. With one the answer is six diamonds. The rest of your hand is irrelevant, you have been asked a specific question so you must answer.

Some simple conventions

1) BARON AND FLINT OVER 2NT

Traditional methods of responding to a 2NT opening are that three clubs is Stayman, asking for a four-card major, while three diamonds, three hearts and three spades are all natural, showing at least a five-card suit and the strength for game. There are two potential weaknesses in this scheme. Firstly, that when one hand is known to be very strong there is the possibility of slam, in which case finding a 4-4 fit in a minor suit could prove just as valuable as in a major. Secondly, if responder has a long suit in a very weak hand he has no weakness take-out bid available. He has to just pass when the hand would probably be better played in his suit. Baron and Flint are two conventional ways of attempting to overcome these weaknesses.

Baron

Using Baron, the three club response to 2NT simply asks opener for his cheapest four-card suit, rather than specifically a major. The idea is that each player in turn bids his cheapest four-card suit until a fit is found — if there is one. So, for example, with four diamonds and four spades, opener rebids three diamonds rather than three spades, and we may get an auction like this:

2NT	3♣(i)
3◇(ii)	3♡(iii)
3♠(iv)	4♠(v)

    (i) Baron
    (ii) lowest four-card suit
    (iii) likewise
    (iv) another suit
    (v) good, so have I

The only proviso is that opener should not be the first one to go beyond 3NT, in case partner was only looking for a major-suit fit for game and did not have the strength to consider a slam. An auction such as:

2NT	3♣
3♡	3♠
3NT	4♣

suggests that responder is interested in slam, otherwise he would have settled for 3NT, rather than look for a club fit. Five clubs is very high for two balanced hands to go.

Flint

Flint is a way of giving responder a weakness response when he holds a long suit. It utilises the three diamond response to 2NT and requests opener to bid three hearts almost whatever his hand. The scheme is as follows:

2NT	3♢	
3♡	Pass	weak hand with long hearts, e.g.

              ♠ 73
              ♡ J 6 5 4 3 2
              ♢ 9 7
              ♣ 8 6 5

             3♠   weak hand with long spades, asks opener to pass, e.g.

              ♠ J 6 5 4 3 2
              ♡ 73
              ♢ 97
              ♣ 8 6 3

             3NT   not forcing, but showing some slam interest and a diamond suit — a hand which would rather have never heard of Flint, e.g.

              ♠ 10 9 5
              ♡ 9 7 4
              ♢ A Q 10 7 3
              ♣ A 6

As I say, opener is normally expected to do as he is told and bid three hearts. If, however, he has a maximum hand with really good heart support, he may wish to have a shot at game even opposite a weak hand. In that case he should bid 2NT – 3♢ – 3♠, saying "If your suit is spades please pass, but if it is hearts I'm willing to go to game." Were opener willing to try for game whichever major partner held, he could bid 2NT – 3♢ – 4♡ to force the partnership to the game level. For example, bid 2NT – 3♢ – 4♡ with:

                 ♠ K Q J 2
                 ♡ A Q J 4
                 ♢ A K Q
                 ♣ 4 2

where game is unlikely to be worse than on the heart finesse, whichever major responder has.

The other responses to 2NT: three or four of a major, 4NT, etc, retain their normal meanings, just as if you were using standard methods throughout.

2) SWISS

Swiss is an artificial bid which is used to show a good raise to game over partner's one heart or one spade opening bid. What is the need for Swiss, you ask? Does not an immediate game raise, 1♡ – 4♡ or 1♠ – 4♠, showing 13–15 points, do the job perfectly adequately?

Up to a point it does, and when we start out in this game it is the best and simplest way of doing things. As we progress, however, and start to think about slams, we find that a sequence which begins 1♠ –4♠ leaves very little room for exploration, if the opener has a strong hand. Swiss gives a little more room.

There are several versions of the convention. What they all have in common is that they utilise two bids which you would never wish to use in a natural sense, namely one of a major – four clubs/four diamonds, to show a high-card raise to game in the major. Perhaps the simplest version is to say that 1♡/1♠ – 4♣ shows 13–16 points but four poor trumps, while 1♡/1♠ – 4♢ shows 13–16 points but promises good trumps. The usual definition of good trumps being at least two of the top three honours, or any three honours. e.g. bid 1♡ – 4♣ with:

> ♠ A J 7
> ♡ Q 7 6 3
> ♢ A Q 10 4
> ♣ 7 3

but 1♡ – 4♢ with:

> ♠ Q 7 3
> ♡ A Q 10 4
> ♢ A J 3 2
> ♣ 10 4

Not only does this scheme allow responder to say something about the quality of his trumps, but it also leaves a little extra space for opener to start cue-bidding, if he is interested. The space gained may not look very much, but it is surprising how useful even a couple of extra bids can be.

If all high-card raises to four of a major are going to be shown via Swiss, that leaves an immediate 1♡ – 4♡ and 1♠ – 4♠ as a distributional raise, based on good trumps and shape. Because it is limited in high cards, opener will rarely carry on towards slam. Sometimes responder may even bid 1♠ – 4♠ on a hand where he does not really expect to make game — e.g.

♠ K J 10 7 3
♡ 6
♢ 8 4
♣ Q 9 6 3 2

This is a sort of each-way bet, maybe four spades will make, but if not it could still be a good save against a contract the other way. Remember, if one side has a big fit, the other side must have a fit as well. You are sufficiently short of high cards that you cannot be certain that the deal actually belongs to your side. If you leap straight to game, you will make it very tough for your opponents to find any contract they may have on, in much the same way as when you open the bidding at the three level you are pre-empting them out of the auction.

3) ONE OF A SUIT - DOUBLE - 2NT

We have mentioned several times that whenever one side has a trump fit so will the other. If an auction becomes competitive, i.e. both sides are bidding, the trick is to make it difficult for your opponents to get together. One such situation is when partner opens the bidding and the next hand makes a take-out double. If you can support partner's suit, you should strain to do so at as high a level as possible, as you may then manage to shut out the fourth player completely.

Caution should be shown when vulnerable as you could suffer a serious penalty if you overdo things, but after 1♡ – Double, one might reasonably bid two hearts on:

♠ J 3
♡ Q J 6 2
♢ 7 4 3
♣ 8 7 6 2

instead of passing, as you would without the double. With:

> ♠ 3
> ♡ Q J 7 6
> ◇ Q 5 4 3 2
> ♣ J 6 2

bid three hearts instead of two hearts, and bid four hearts with:

> ♠ 3
> ♡ Q J 7 6 3
> ◇ Q 5 4 3 2
> ♣ J 6

If you are going to bid three hearts pre-emptively on the second hand, what do you do with a genuine three heart bid such as:

> ♠ A 10 3
> ♡ K J 7 6
> ◇ Q J 4 2
> ♣ 6 5

This hand is worth a game invitation, but if you bid three hearts, partner will expect something more like the example above with less high-card strength. The solution is to respond 2NT. This is an artificial bid which says "I have a genuine three heart bid based on high cards and am inviting game." Opener may now bid three hearts as a sign off with a minimum opener or bid four hearts with a little to spare. But doesn't a 2NT response normally show about 11–12 HCPs *without* support for partner? What do you respond with, say:

> ♠ A J 3
> ♡ J 4 2
> ◇ Q J 7 6
> ♣ Q 10 8

The answer is that all good balanced hands with less than four-card support for partner start off by redoubling, remember? So over the double, a 2NT response is completely redundant in a natural sense and can be used as suggested above, to allow you to bid your invitational supporting hands properly, while making life tough for your opponents with the more pre-emptive immediate raises.

QUIZ SIXTEEN
Conventions

Assuming that you are playing all the conventions discussed in this section, what would be your next bid with each of these hands?

1)	♠ J76432		**West**	**East**
	♡ 84		2NT	?
	◇ 72			
	♣ 963			

2)	♠ J843		**West**	**East**
	♡ AK4		2NT	?
	◇ KJ62			
	♣ 103			

3)	♠ 63		**West**	**East**
	♡ 1094		2NT	?
	◇ AJ1074			
	♣ AJ2			

4)	♠ A10873		**West**	**East**
	♡ J104		2NT	?
	◇ 6			
	♣ 9753			

5)	♠ AK4		**West**	**East**
	♡ Q7		2NT	3◇
	◇ KJ83		?	
	♣ AK64			

6)	♠ AQ74		**West**	**East**
	♡ AK3		2NT	3♣
	◇ QJ64		?	
	♣ AJ			

7)	♠ KQJ		**West**	**East**
	♡ AJ64		2NT	3♣
	◇ AQ73		3◇	3♠
	♣ A3		?	

8) ♠ A K 4
    ♡ A J 10 4
    ♢ K 3
    ♣ 7 6 5 2

West	East
1♡	?

9) ♠ A K Q
    ♡ J 7 6 3
    ♢ A J 4
    ♣ 7 3 2

West	East
1♡	?

10) ♠ 7
    ♡ K 10 7 6
    ♢ A Q 10 5 3
    ♣ 7 4 2

West	East
1♡	?

11) ♠ A K Q J
    ♡ 10 7 6 4
    ♢ 6 4
    ♣ A K Q

West	East
1♡	4♣
?	

12) ♠ A 4
    ♡ K Q 7 6 4
    ♢ A K 10 6 3
    ♣ 2

West	East
1♡	4♣
?	

13) ♠ K 4 2
    ♡ A Q 7 3
    ♢ A Q 6 3
    ♣ 7 2

West	East
1♡	4♢
4♠	?

14) ♠ A J 3
    ♡ A Q 7 2
    ♢ 7 4
    ♣ 9 7 6 2

West	North	East	South
1♡	Dble	?	

15) ♠ K 4
    ♡ J 10 3 2
    ♢ 7 6 3 2
    ♣ 10 5 4

West	North	East	South
1♡	Dble	?	

16) ♠ 10
    ♡ J 10 3 2
    ◇ K J 7 4 2
    ♣ 7 6 2

West	North	East	South
1♡	Dble	?	

17) ♠ A 3
    ♡ K J 10 7 3
    ◇ A K 3
    ♣ 7 4 2

West	North	East	South
1♡	Dble	3♡	Pass
?			

18) ♠ A 3
    ♡ K J 10 7 3
    ◇ A K 3
    ♣ 7 4 2

West	North	East	South
1♡	Dble	2NT	Pass
?			

SOLUTIONS TO QUIZ SIXTEEN
Conventions

1) ♠ J76432   West   East
    ♡ 84   2NT   ?
    ◇ 72
    ♣ 963

Three diamonds. Three spades would be forcing, partner could not pass, and what you want with such a weak hand is to be allowed to play in three spades. The solution is to bid three diamonds, Flint, which asks partner to bid three hearts but now, when you follow up with three spades, you can expect him to leave you there.

2) ♠ J843   West   East
    ♡ AK4   2NT   ?
    ◇ KJ62
    ♣ 103

Three clubs. You have the values for a raise to 4NT, invitational, but even opposite a minimum, there could be a slam if you can find a 4-4 fit. A Baron three clubs, asking for four-card suits up the line, is a better choice. You can always raise to 4NT later, if no fit presents itself.

3) ♠ 63   West   East
    ♡ 1094   2NT   ?
    ◇ AJ1074
    ♣ AJ2

Three diamonds. This is Flint and partner will usually convert to three hearts, as requested. When you follow up with 3NT, however, he will realise that you actually had diamonds all along and were making a mild slam try.

4) ♠ A10873   West   East
    ♡ J104   2NT   ?
    ◇ 6
    ♣ 9753

Three spades. When you have a long major suit and game values, you just bid it as normal. Flint is only used with weak hands. Over three spades, partner will choose between four spades and 3NT.

5)   ♠ A K 4   **West**   **East**
      ♡ Q 7   2NT   3◇
      ◇ K J 8 3   ?
      ♣ A K 6 4

Three hearts. Three diamonds was Flint, asking you to bid three hearts. With no exceptional heart support, you should do as requested.

6)   ♠ A Q 7 4   **West**   **East**
      ♡ A K 3   2NT   3♣
      ◇ Q J 6 4   ?
      ♣ A J

Three diamonds. Playing Stayman, you would have bid three spades, your four-card major. Playing Baron, you bid your cheapest four-card suit first, the spades will keep.

7)   ♠ K Q J   **West**   **East**
      ♡ A J 6 4   2NT   3♣
      ◇ A Q 7 3   3◇   3♠
      ♣ A 3   ?

3NT. Three clubs was Baron and three spades showed a four-card suit. It also denied four hearts, as partner would have bid his cheaper suit if he had a choice. There is therefore no point in bidding your hearts. The general rule is that opener should not be the first to go beyond 3NT, unless it is to agree partner's suit as trumps.

8)   ♠ A K 4   **West**   **East**
      ♡ A J 10 4   1♡   ?
      ◇ K 3
      ♣ 7 6 5 2

Four diamonds. With plenty of high-card strength, you would be quite happy to cooperate if partner were to look for a slam. A potentially pre-emptive raise to four hearts would not be appropriate. Instead, try a Swiss four diamond bid, showing a good raise to four hearts with about 13–16 HCPs and good trumps.

9)	♠ A K Q	West	East
	♡ J 7 6 3	1♡	?
	◇ A J 4		
	♣ 7 3 2		

Four clubs. Much the same as the previous example, except that your trumps are poor, so you bid four clubs instead of four diamonds.

10)	♠ 7	West	East
	♡ K 1 0 7 6	1♡	?
	◇ A Q 1 0 5 3		
	♣ 7 4 2		

Four hearts. You cannot be certain of making this, but it is worth the slight stretch to try to shut out the opposition, who appear to have a big spade fit.

11)	♠ A K Q J	West	East
	♡ 1 0 7 6 4	1♡	4♣
	◇ 6 4	?	
	♣ A K Q		

Four hearts. Partner has shown a good raise to four hearts and with your own high-card strength, it is very tempting to try for a slam. However, four clubs also shows weakish trumps, so with your own very poor trumps you should resist the temptation. There will surely prove to be at least two trump losers.

12)	♠ A 4	West	East
	♡ K Q 7 6 4	1♡	4♣
	◇ A K 1 0 6 3	?	
	♣ 2		

Four diamonds. Opposite a four club Swiss bid, you have to be interested in slam, your own trumps being sufficiently strong that you need not worry that partner's are not. A four diamond cue-bid is the best way to continue, then partner will show his control, if he has one, and you can take it from there.

13) ♠ K42
     ♡ AQ73
     ◇ AQ63
     ♣ 72

West	East
1♡	4◇
4♠	?

Five diamonds. Your four diamonds was Swiss, showing a good raise to
four hearts with good trumps. That was sufficient to encourage partner to
cue-bid in search of slam and you should in turn cooperate by cue-bidding
your ace of diamonds. Because you have bypassed clubs, you also deny the
ace of that suit.

14) ♠ AJ3
     ♡ AQ72
     ◇ 74
     ♣ 9762

West	North	East	South
1♡	Dble	?	

2NT. You have a genuine invitational raise to three hearts. Over the double
you must bid 2NT and not three hearts, which would show a weaker more
pre-emptive raise.

15) ♠ K4
     ♡ J1032
     ◇ 7632
     ♣ 1054

West	North	East	South
1♡	Dble	?	

Two hearts. Without the double you would have passed, but it is worth the
stretch to get in the way of your opponents, to whom the deal probably
belongs. Partner should understand what you are trying to do, so will not
get carried away.

16) ♠ 10
     ♡ J1032
     ◇ KJ742
     ♣ 762

West	North	East	South
1♡	Dble	?	

Three hearts. A normal two heart raise, but with such poor defence you
should do your best to shut out the fourth hand by jumping. Indeed, while
I would consider it to be overdoing a good thing somewhat, there are players
who would jump all the way to four hearts on this hand.

17) ♠ A 3
♡ KJ1073
◇ AK3
♣ 742

West	North	East	South
1♡	Dble	3♡	Pass
?			

Pass. Partner's three hearts is largely pre-emptive and although you have a little to spare, you should be cautious about raising to game, in case he is really weak.

18) ♠ A 3
♡ KJ1073
◇ AK3
♣ 742

West	North	East	South
1♡	Dble	2NT	Pass
?			

Four hearts. This time, he has promised a genuine raise to three hearts, so you can afford to go on to game just as you would have done after 1♡ – 3♡ without the double.

SECTION FIVE
REVISION PROBLEMS

The conventions discussed in the last section are a matter for individual partnerships to discuss and decide which to play and which to reject. It cannot be assumed that if you sit down opposite a complete stranger he will be using them. However, once you feel confident about basic bidding, they are well worth adding to your armoury and, for the purposes of these final sets of problems, you should assume that you are using everything which we have discussed: Baron over 2NT rather than Stayman, Flint, Swiss, etc.

Revision Quiz One

What would you bid next in each of these sequences?

			West	East
1)	♠ J10732		West	East
	♡ Q63		1♡	1♠
	♢ 72		2♣	?
	♣ KJ4			

			West	East
2)	♠ K10732		West	East
	♡ A4		1♡	1♠
	♢ J63		2♣	?
	♣ AJ2			

			West	East
3)	♠ AQJ63		West	East
	♡ AK74		1♠	4♣
	♢ K8		?	
	♣ 76			

			West	East
4)	♠ J764		West	East
	♡ K1096		1NT	2♣
	♢ AK		2♠	?
	♣ 1063			

			West	East
5)	♠ 7		West	East
	♡ J642		3♡	?
	♢ KQ1064			
	♣ 1083			

			West	East
6)	♠ AJ64		West	East
	♡ K2		1♢	2♣
	♢ KQ976		?	
	♣ 64			

			West	East
7)	♠ A93		West	East
	♡ KJ10874		1♡	2NT
	♢ J4		?	
	♣ Q3			

8)
♠ A K 4
♥ A Q J 3
♦ K 10 7 3
♣ A Q

West	East
2♣	2♦
2NT	3♣
?	

9)
♠ 7 6
♥ A J 10 6 3
♦ K Q 7 4
♣ K 2

West	East
1♥	2♣
?	

10)
♠ A 6 2
♥ 10 7 4
♦ 8 6
♣ K Q 9 8 6

West	East
1♥	2♣
3♦	?

11)
♠ A 10 9
♥ Q 9 8 7 4
♦ Q J 4
♣ J 3

West	East
1♣	1♥
3♣	?

12)
♠ A K Q
♥ A Q J 10 9 6
♦ K 3
♣ K 4

West	East
2♥	4♥
?	

13)
♠ 10 7 4 2
♥ Q J 6 4
♦ K 3
♣ Q 6 2

West	East
1♥	2♥
3♦	?

14)
♠ Q 6 3
♥ A 4
♦ A K 10 6 3
♣ Q 3 2

West	East
1♦	2♠
?	

15)
♠ A Q 6 3
♥ A K Q 10 6 4
♦ K Q
♣ 7

West	East
2♣	2♠
?	

		West	North	East	South
16)	♠ 1083 ♡ J762 ◇ 105 ♣ 8762	3♣	Dble	Pass	?
17)	♠ QJ10983 ♡ 763 ◇ A7 ♣ J4	1♠	Dble	Pass	?
18)	♠ AK64 ♡ 7 ◇ AQJ3 ♣ KQ107	1♡ Pass	Dble ?	2♡	Pass
19)	♠ A10 ♡ Q106 ◇ AQJ32 ♣ KQ4	1◇ ?	Dble	3◇	Pass
20)	♠ AJ43 ♡ KQ10 ◇ K2 ♣ AQJ5	1◇ Pass	Dble ?	Pass	1♠

Solutions to Revision Quiz One

1) ♠ J 10 7 3 2   West   East
    ♡ Q 6 3   1♡   1♠
    ◇ 7 2   2♣   ?
    ♣ K J 4

Two hearts. With a weak hand, you can only choose between partner's suits. With equal length, you return to his first suit, as that will be the longer if they are of unequal length.

2) ♠ K 10 7 3 2   West   East
    ♡ A 4   1♡   1♠
    ◇ J 6 3   2♣   ?
    ♣ A J 2

Two diamonds. This is fourth suit forcing, asking partner to describe his hand further, neither promising nor denying diamonds. This is exactly what you need here, as you have no good bid available to describe your own hand.

3) ♠ A Q J 6 3   West   East
    ♡ A K 7 4   1♠   4♣
    ◇ K 8   ?
    ♣ 7 6

Four hearts. Four clubs was Swiss, showing a good raise to four spades with poor trumps. You have substantial extra values and should look for a slam. The best way is to show your ace of hearts and see if partner can show a useful control in turn.

4) ♠ J 7 6 4   West   East
    ♡ K 10 9 6   1NT   2♣
    ◇ A K   2♠   ?
    ♣ 10 6 3

Three spades. You have found a trump fit as you hoped. Three spades invites game, showing about 11–12 points, and asks partner to bid game with a maximum, but pass with a minimum.

5)	♠ 7	West	East
	♡ J642	3♡	?
	◇ KQ1064		
	♣ 1083		

Four hearts. Partner is weak, but has a good seven-card heart suit. It is not that you expect to make game, unless you get very lucky, but that you are sure that your opponents can make at least a game elsewhere, if they get together. Raising to four hearts makes life that much more difficult for them.

6)	♠ AJ64	West	East
	♡ K2	1◇	2♣
	◇ KQ976	?	
	♣ 64		

Two diamonds. It would be nice to be able to bid the spades to give partner a choice, but you are not strong enough. Two spades would push the bidding up a level and would be a reverse, showing about 16 plus points. The only alternative is to rebid the diamonds.

7)	♠ A93	West	East
	♡ KJ10874	1♡	2NT
	◇ J4	?	
	♣ Q3		

Three hearts. 2NT was a limit bid showing 11–12 points and a balanced hand. With a completely minimum opening, you are not strong enough to bid game. One possibility would be to pass, but with your long suit it is likely to be safer to play in hearts than in no-trumps. Bid three hearts, which partner should usually pass.

8)	♠ AK4	West	East
	♡ AQJ3	2♣	2◇
	◇ K1073	2NT	3♣
	♣ AQ	?	

Three diamonds. Three clubs was Baron, asking for four-card suits upwards.

9)	♠ 76	West	East
	♡ AJ1063	1♡	2♣
	◇ KQ74	?	
	♣ K2		

Two diamonds. With 5-4 you do best to bid the second suit where possible, to give partner a choice.

10) ♠ A 6 2
     ♡ 1074
     ◇ 86
     ♣ K Q 9 8 6

West	East
1♡	2♣
3◇	?

Three hearts. Three diamonds, being a jump bid, showed a strong hand and was forcing to game. It also promised at least five hearts so, despite your spade stopper, you are better to support his first suit. Three hearts shows a minimum hand.

11) ♠ A 109
     ♡ Q9874
     ◇ Q J 4
     ♣ J 3

West	East
1♣	1♡
3♣	?

3NT. Partner has shown a good six-card suit and 16 plus points, so you must bid again. With a pretty balanced hand and stoppers in the unbid suits, no-trumps is the obvious choice.

12) ♠ A K Q
     ♡ A Q J 1096
     ◇ K 3
     ♣ K 4

West	East
2♡	4♡
?	

Pass. Partner likes hearts and has positive values but has denied holding an ace, so there can be no slam.

13) ♠ 10742
     ♡ Q J 64
     ◇ K 3
     ♣ Q 6 2

West	East
1♡	2♡
3◇	?

Four hearts. Three diamonds was a game try in hearts. As you are near maximum and have a good diamond holding, you should accept the invitation.

14) ♠ Q 63
     ♡ A 4
     ◇ A K 1063
     ♣ Q 32

West	East
1◇	2♠
?	

Three spades. Over one spade you would have rebid 1NT, but now that partner has shown a powerful suit, you have ample to support him immediately. This will greatly simplify things, if he wishes to look for a slam.

15) ♠ A Q 6 3
    ♡ A K Q 10 6 4
    ◇ K Q
    ♣ 7

West	East
2♣	2♠
?	

4NT. There are only three possible losers, the two aces and the king of spades. Blackwood should get you to the right level. Sign off in five spades if he has no ace; bid six spades opposite one; ask for kings if he shows two, as seven may be on.

16) ♠ 1083
    ♡ J 7 6 2
    ◇ 10 5
    ♣ 8 7 6 2

West	North	East	South
3♣	Dble	Pass	?

Three hearts. The double was for take-out, so you must bid as otherwise you leave the opposition in a contract which they are all too likely to make. Bid your longest suit and cross your fingers.

17) ♠ Q J 10 9 8 3
    ♡ 7 6 3
    ◇ A 7
    ♣ J 4

West	North	East	South
1♠	Dble	Pass	?

Pass. This is the rare hand with which you pass partner's take-out double, not because you are too weak to bid, but because you have a positive desire to defend against one spade doubled.

18) ♠ A K 6 4
    ♡ 7
    ◇ A Q J 3
    ♣ K Q 10 7

West	North	East	South
1♡	Dble	2♡	Pass
Pass	?		

Double. This is a second take-out double, showing extra strength and asking partner to pick a suit.

19) ♠ A 10
    ♡ Q 10 6
    ◇ A Q J 3 2
    ♣ K Q 4

West	North	East	South
1◇	Dble	3◇	Pass
?			

3NT. Even though three diamonds was essentially pre-emptive, you have so many high cards that you must try a game contract. With your balanced hand, 3NT could prove easier than five diamonds, despite the good diamond fit.

20) ♠ A J 4 3

     ♡ K Q 10

     ◇ K 2

     ♣ A Q J 5

West	North	East	South
1◇	Dble	Pass	1♠
Pass	?		

Three spades. Even opposite 0–7 points, there must be a chance of game with your strong hand. Three spades is not forcing but strongly encourages partner to bid the game.

Revision Quiz Two

In each case what was the meaning of the last bid in these sequences?

1)	West	East
	1♡	1♠
	2NT	

2)	West	East
	1♣	1♠
	2♢	

3)	West	East
	1♣	3♣

4)	West	East
	1♠	3NT

5)	West	East
	1♠	4♢
	4♠	

6)	West	East
	1NT	2♣
	2♢	2NT

7)	West	East
	2NT	3♣
	3♢	3♠

8)	West	East
	1♢	1♠
	3♠	

9)	West	East
	2♣	2NT

10)	West	East
	1♣	1♢
	1♡	1♠
	2♠	

11)	West	East
	2♠	2NT
	3♡	3♠

12)	West	East
	1♠	2♣
	3♡	

13)	West	East
	1♡	3♡
	4♣	

14)	West	East
	1♢	2♠

15)	West	North	East	South
	1♡	Dble	Pass	2♡

16)	West	North	East	South
	1♢	Dble	Pass	1♠
	Pass	2♡		

17)	West	North	East	South
	1♡	1NT	Pass	2♣

18)	West	North	East	South
	3♢	Dble	Pass	4♢

19)	West	North	East	South
	1♡	Dble	2NT	Pass
	3♡			

20)	West	North	East	South
	1♡	1♠	2NT	

Solutions to Revision Quiz Two

	West	**East**
1)	1♡	1♠
	2NT	

The 2NT rebid shows a balanced hand with 17–18 HCPs. It denies four-card spade support.

2)	1♣	1♠
	2◇	

Two diamonds shows four diamonds, at least five clubs, and a strong hand — 16 plus points. Why a strong hand? Because if partner wishes to give preference to the first suit, clubs, he has to go to the three-level to do so, making two diamonds a reverse.

3)	1♣	3♣

A limit bid, roughly 10–12 points and at least four-card club support. It will tend to deny a decent four-card major suit, as partner would look for a fit in a major, before settling for a minor.

4)	1♠	3NT

A completely balanced hand with less than four spades, and 13–15 HCPs.

5)	1♠	4◇
	4♠	

Four diamonds was Swiss showing a good raise to four spades. When opener rebids four spades he is just signing off, i.e. saying that he is not interested in slam.

6)	1NT	2♣
	2◇	2NT

The fact that responder used Stayman on the way, does not affect the meaning of a raise to 2NT, it still shows 11–12 points and invites 3NT.

	West	**East**
7)	2NT	3♣
	3♢	3♠

Three clubs was Baron. Three spades shows a four-card spade suit and denies four hearts.

8)	1♢	1♠
	3♠	

This shows four-card spade support and around 16–18 total points — an above minimum opening, but not quite enough to bid game opposite what might be only a 6 or 7 point response. With less you would have bid only two spades.

9)	2♣	2NT

A balanced hand with about 7–9 scattered points. It is forcing to at least game, as two clubs showed a very powerful hand.

10)	1♣	1♢
	1♡	1♠
	2♠	

One spade was fourth suit forcing, asking opener to describe his hand further. The simple raise to two spades shows a minimum hand, roughly 12–14 points, with four spades. Opener must be either 4-4-1-4 or 4-4-0-5 shape.

11)	2♠	2NT
	3♡	3♠

Two spades was forcing and 2NT showed a weak hand. Three spades simply says that responder prefers spades to hearts, but is very weak. If he had anything useful, he would have bid four spades.

12)	1♠	2♣
	3♡	

Opener has at least five spades, at least four hearts, and 16 or more points. With a weaker hand he would not have jumped. Three hearts forces partner to bid again.

	West	**East**
13)	1♡	3♡
	4♣	

Hearts have been agreed as trumps and four clubs commits the partnership to game, so it is a cue-bid showing a club control and slam interest. It also denies first-round control of spades, as opener would always bid his lowest first-round control.

14)   1◇   2♠

A jump shift response shows a powerful suit and usually at least 16 points.

	West	**North**	**East**	**South**
15)	1♡	Dble	Pass	2♡

The double was for take-out and the one suit responder could not want to play in is hearts. If he had such good hearts, he would just have passed out one heart doubled and collected a penalty. The cue-bid of the opponents' suit says that he wants to play in game, but does not know which game. It forces partner to keep the bidding open until game is reached.

16)	1◇	Dble	Pass	1♠
	Pass	2♡		

The double was for take-out and partner chose spades. The only reason to overrule him would be that the doubler did not actually have support for every suit, but had a long heart suit. Why then did he not simply overcall one heart? He must be too strong to do so.

17)   1♡   1NT   Pass   2♣

This is Stayman, just as over a 1NT opening bid.

18)   3◇   Dble   Pass   4◇

As in example 15), a cue-bid in the opponents' suit in response to the double shows that he wants to play in game, but does not know in which suit to play. The doubler should usually pick his longer major in response to the cue-bid.

	West	**North**	**East**	**South**
19)	1♡	Dble	2NT	Pass
	3♡			

2NT showed a genuine raise to three hearts. Three hearts is a sign off, showing a minimum hand which is too weak to bid game.

20)	1♡	1♠	2NT

Just as without the intervention, 11 or 12 HCPs and a balanced hand. One important difference, however, is that it is an absolute must to have at least one and preferably two sure spade stops, now that the suit has been bid by an opponent. That is the suit they are sure to lead against no-trumps.

Revision Quiz Three

Suggest a good bidding sequence for these pairs of hands. West to bid first.

	West	East
1)	♠ 3	♠ A J 6 3
	♡ A Q 10 7 3	♡ K 8 4 2
	◇ A K 6 4	◇ 7 2
	♣ Q 6 3	♣ K 5 4
2)	♠ K Q 6 4	♠ J 7 2
	♡ A 7 3	♡ K 10 8
	◇ J 10 4	◇ K Q 3
	♣ A Q 3	♣ K 5 4 2
3)	♠ 7 3	♠ Q 9 8 6 4
	♡ A	♡ 7 6 4 2
	◇ K J 9 6 3	◇ Q 8
	♣ A 10 8 7 4	♣ K 3
4)	♠ A 6 3	♠ Q 4 2
	♡ K Q 7 6 2	♡ 8
	◇ 8	◇ K J 10 7 6 4
	♣ A J 7 4	♣ 10 8 3
5)	♠ J 10 7 3	♠ K Q 6 4
	♡ A Q 6 2	♡ K 7
	◇ A K	◇ 10 8 4 2
	♣ 10 9 4	♣ K 8 3
6)	♠ 9	♠ A Q 8 3 2
	♡ K 10 9 8 6	♡ A 5
	◇ K J 4	◇ 10 6 2
	♣ A J 10 3	♣ K Q 2
7)	♠ K Q 8 2	♠ 7 3
	♡ A J	♡ 10 8 6 4 3 2
	◇ A Q 7 4	◇ 9 6 2
	♣ A J 2	♣ 8 4

	West	East
8)	♠ A Q J 10 8 3	♠ K 9 4 2
	♡ 7 2	♡ K Q 8
	◇ K Q	◇ A 10 6 3
	♣ A K Q	♣ 7 2
9)	♠ A Q J	♠ 7 6 3 2
	♡ A K 5 2	♡ 8 7 4
	◇ K J 3	◇ 10 8 6
	♣ A Q 10	♣ 9 8 5
10)	♠ A Q J 3	♠ 10 8 6 4
	♡ A K 10	♡ Q 3
	◇ K	◇ J 8 7 5 2
	♣ A K J 6 4	♣ 7 2
11)	♠ A 3	♠ 8 6 5
	♡ A K Q 10 4	♡ 7
	◇ K Q J 7 3	◇ 10 8 6 5 4 2
	♣ 8	♣ J 7 4
12)	♠ A K 10 7 3	♠ 6 4
	♡ 9	♡ A 10 8 4 2
	◇ A J 5	◇ K Q 7
	♣ A J 8 4	♣ Q 6 3
13)	♠ K 7 2	♠ Q 6 3
	♡ A Q 10 4	♡ K 5 3 2
	◇ K Q 3	◇ 7 6
	♣ A 6 2	♣ J 8 5 4
14)	♠ J 3	♠ A 4
	♡ A K 7 6 2	♡ 9 3
	◇ 10 4	◇ 8 7 6 5
	♣ A J 8 3	♣ K 10 7 6 5
15)	South opens 3◇	
	♠ A J 6 2	♠ K Q 5
	♡ A K 7 3	♡ Q 10 8 6 4
	◇ 9	◇ J 8
	♣ K 8 6 2	♣ Q 9 3

	West	East
16)	South opens 1♡	
	♠ A K 10 6 4	♠ Q 9 2
	♡ A 3	♡ 8 7 5
	◇ J 8 4 2	◇ A K 3
	♣ 10 3	♣ 9 6 4 2
17)	South opens 1♠	
	♠ A Q 3	♠ 8 4
	♡ Q 4	♡ J 10 7 5 3 2
	◇ A J 7 4	◇ Q 3
	♣ K 10 6 3	♣ 7 5 2
18)	South opens 1♡	
	♠ A Q 8 2	♠ K 6 3
	♡ 7	♡ A J 10 4
	◇ A K 6 3	◇ Q 7 2
	♣ K 9 7 2	♣ J 10 4
19)	South opens 1♣	
	♠ A Q 3 2	♠ K 9 7 4
	♡ K J 4	♡ A 10 8 3
	◇ A 9 6 3 2	◇ Q 5
	♣ 7	♣ A 6 3
20)	South opens 1NT	
	♠ K Q J 4	♠ A 3 2
	♡ A K 7	♡ 10 8
	◇ Q 10 7	◇ K 6 4 3
	♣ K 9 8	♣ 10 6 3 2

Solutions to Revision Quiz Three

	West	East	West	East
1)	♠ 3	♠ A J 6 3	1♡	3♡
	♡ A Q 10 7 3	♡ K 8 4 2	4♡	Pass
	◇ A K 6 4	◇ 7 2		
	♣ Q 6 3	♣ K 5 4		

Three hearts is a limit raise, showing around 10–12 points and inviting game. As West has extra values, he goes on to game.

	West	East	West	East
2)	♠ K Q 6 4	♠ J 7 2	1♠	2NT
	♡ A 7 3	♡ K 10 8	3NT	Pass
	◇ J 10 4	◇ K Q 3		
	♣ A Q 3	♣ K 5 4 2		

West opens one spade because he is too strong for 1NT. The 2NT response shows 11–12 HCPs in a balanced hand. West knows that there are sufficient points for game and, as both hands are balanced, raises to 3NT.

	West	East	West	East
3)	♠ 7 3	♠ Q 9 8 6 4	1◇	1♠
	♡ A	♡ 7 6 4 2	2♣	2◇
	◇ K J 9 6 3	◇ Q 8	Pass	
	♣ A 10 8 7 4	♣ K 3		

West opens the higher of his two five-card suits, then gives partner a choice by bidding the second suit. East is only strong enough to choose between partner's suits as cheaply as possible, so he goes back to the first one, in case they are of unequal length. The spades are too weak to consider bidding a second time.

	West	East	West	East
4)	♠ A 6 3	♠ Q 4 2	1♡	1NT
	♡ K Q 7 6 2	♡ 8	2♣	2◇
	◇ 8	◇ K J 10 7 6 4	Pass	
	♣ A J 7 4	♣ 10 8 3		

East is too weak to bid two diamonds over one heart, so he responds 1NT. West shows his second suit, as usual with 5-4, and East takes the opportunity to bid his diamonds. East must have a long suit, as otherwise he would just have chosen one of his partner's suits, and he is of course limited to 6–8 points by his initial response. West passes, trusting partner to have a lot of diamonds.

	West	East	West	East
5)	♠ J1073	♠ KQ64	1NT	2♣
	♡ AQ62	♡ K7	2♡	2NT
	◇ AK	◇ 10842	4♠	Pass
	♣ 1094	♣ K83		

West opens 1NT, 12–14 balanced and, rather than just raise to 2NT, East checks for a 4-4 spade fit on the way, via Stayman. Two hearts shows four hearts and, not having got the response he was looking for, East now bids 2NT, 11–12 balanced. With a maximum, West accepts the invitation to game, but bids four spades rather than 3NT because he knows East must have four spades to have used Stayman, when he clearly does not have hearts.

	West	East	West	East
6)	♠ 9	♠ AQ832	1♡	1♠
	♡ K10986	♡ A5	2♣	2◇
	◇ KJ4	◇ 1062	2NT	3NT
	♣ AJ103	♣ KQ2	Pass	

Over two clubs, East has no good bid to describe his hand, so he bids the fourth suit. This is forcing but does not necessarily say anything about diamonds. When West now bids 2NT, showing a minimum opening with a diamond stopper, East has the information he needs. There is no trump fit but every suit is covered, so 3NT should be the right game.

	West	East	West	East
7)	♠ KQ82	♠ 73	2NT	3◇
	♡ AJ	♡ 1086432	3♡	Pass
	◇ AQ74	◇ 962		
	♣ AJ2	♣ 84		

West opens 2NT to show 20–22 HCPs and a balanced hand, and East is too weak to be interested in game. He knows that the hand will be better played in his long suit. Accordingly he uses Flint, three diamonds asking opener to bid three hearts, and is able to pass the response.

	West	East	West	East
8)	♠ AQJ1083	♠ K942	2♠	3♠
	♡ 72	♡ KQ8	4♣	4◇
	◇ KQ	◇ A1063	4♠	6♠
	♣ AKQ	♣ 72	Pass	

Two spades shows a long strong suit and about eight or more playing tricks. Three spades promises spade support, positive values, and usually at least one ace. Four clubs and four diamonds are cue-bids, showing control cards in those suits. West has to sign off in four spades, as he does not have a heart control. With his heart control and extra strength, however, East now goes on to the slam.

	West	East	West	East
9)	♠ A Q J	♠ 7632	2♣	2◇
	♡ A K 5 2	♡ 874	2NT	Pass
	◇ K J 3	◇ 1086		
	♣ A Q 10	♣ 985		

Two clubs followed by 2NT shows a hand too good to open 2NT, 23–24 HCPs in a balanced hand. Two diamonds was a negative response, showing 0–6 points and having nothing to do with diamonds. 2NT is the one rebid which responder is allowed to pass. As East has absolutely nothing, he avails himself of the opportunity.

	West	East	West	East
10)	♠ A Q J 3	♠ 10864	2♣	2◇
	♡ A K 10	♡ Q 3	3♣	3◇
	◇ K	◇ J 8752	3♠	4♠
	♣ A K J 64	♣ 72	Pass	

Two clubs shows a very powerful hand and two diamonds is the weak response. Now both players start to bid their suits in the normal way, longest first, remembering that they have not yet actually shown any suits. West bids clubs first, and East diamonds. When West rebids three spades, a fit is found, so East raises to game. Though he has a very big hand, West should not now look for slam, as he has already promised a big hand. East could have bid more than four spades had he wanted to.

	West	East	West	East
11)	♠ A 3	♠ 865	2♡	2NT
	♡ A K Q 104	♡ 7	3◇	4◇
	◇ K Q J 73	◇ 1086542	5◇	Pass
	♣ 8	♣ J 74		

When West opens at the two level to show an eight-trick hand, East must respond and starts with 2NT, to show a poor hand. Once West bids diamonds, however, East's hand is no longer worthless and he shows a little something by raising to four diamonds. As West has a little to spare for his bidding to date, he accepts the invitation.

	West	East	West	East
12)	♠ A K 10 7 3	♠ 64	1♠	2♡
	♡ 9	♡ A 10 8 4 2	3♣	3NT
	◇ A J 5	◇ K Q 7	Pass	
	♣ A J 8 4	♣ Q 6 3		

West's high level reverse with three clubs takes the bidding higher, so shows 16 plus points. This means that East must bid again and, with no guarantee of an eight-card fit anywhere but a good stop in the unbid suit, 3NT is the obvious choice.

	West	East	West	East
13)	♠ K 7 2	♠ Q 6 3	1♡	2♡
	♡ A Q 10 4	♡ K 5 3 2	2NT	3♡
	◇ K Q 3	◇ 7 6	Pass	
	♣ A 6 2	♣ J 8 5 4		

Hearts having been agreed upon as trumps, 2NT was a try for game showing a strong balanced hand. With a minimum two heart response, East declines the invitation and just goes back to the known fit as cheaply as possible.

	West	East	West	East
14)	♠ J 3	♠ A 4	1♡	1NT
	♡ A K 7 6 2	♡ 9 3	2♣	3♣
	◇ 10 4	◇ 8 7 6 5	Pass	
	♣ A J 8 3	♣ K 10 7 6 5		

East is too weak for two clubs, so must respond 1NT. When West rebids two clubs, however, East's hand is so much improved by the big club fit, that he should raise, rather than just pass. West passes three clubs, as he has nothing to spare and cannot envisage game.

	West	East
15)	♠ A J 6 2	♠ K Q 5
	♡ A K 7 3	♡ Q 10 8 6 4
	◇ 9	◇ J 8
	♣ K 8 6 2	♣ Q 9 3

South	West	North	East
3◇	Dble	Pass	4♡
All Pass			

With his good hand, West must bid over the pre-empt, but there is nothing he can overcall, so he makes a take-out double instead. This asks East for his longest suit, but it also asks him how good his hand is. With 10 HCPs and a five-card suit, East jumps to game to show that he is not just bidding because he was forced to do so.

16)   ♠ A K 10 6 4   ♠ Q 9 2
       ♡ A 3   ♡ 8 7 5
       ◇ J 8 4 2   ◇ A K 3
       ♣ 10 3   ♣ 9 6 4 2

South	West	North	East
1♡	1♠	Pass	2♠
All Pass			

With a good five-card suit West overcalls one spade. East's raise to two spades shows about 6–10 points. Because an overcall promises a five-card suit, it is quite permissible to support with only three cards. West has no reason to think of game opposite a single raise, so passes.

17)   ♠ A Q 3   ♠ 8 4
       ♡ Q 4   ♡ J 10 7 5 3 2
       ◇ A J 7 4   ◇ Q 3
       ♣ K 10 6 3   ♣ 7 5 2

South	West	North	East
1♠	1NT	Pass	2♡
All Pass			

With 15–17 HCPs and a sure spade stopper in a balanced hand, West overcalls 1NT. East prefers to play in his long suit, just as he would have done had be been facing a 1NT opening bid, so he bids two hearts. This is a weakness take-out and compels partner to pass.

18)   ♠ A Q 8 2   ♠ K 6 3
       ♡ 7   ♡ A J 10 4
       ◇ A K 6 3   ◇ Q 7 2
       ♣ K 9 7 2   ♣ J 10 4

South	West	North	East
1♡	Dble	Pass	2NT
Pass	3NT	All Pass	

With the other three suits, West doubles for take-out, and East responds 2NT to show a balanced 11–12 points with a strong heart holding. West has sufficient extra to go on to game and should accept partner's decision that no-trumps is the place to be.

19) ♠ A Q 3 2 ♠ K 9 7 4
       ♡ K J 4 ♡ A 1 0 8 3
       ◇ A 9 6 3 2 ◇ Q 5
       ♣ 7 ♣ A 6 3

South	West	North	East
1♣	Dble	Pass	2♣
Pass	2◇	Pass	2♡
Pass	2♠	Pass	4♠
All Pass			

West is quite happy with whatever suit his partner chooses, so double is more flexible than a one diamond overcall. In response, East has enough strength for game, but has no idea which game he should bid. He cue-bids the opponents' suit to say so. Each player in turn now bids his suits until a fit is found and, when West bids spades, East is able to jump to game.

20) ♠ K Q J 4 ♠ A 3 2
       ♡ A K 7 ♡ 1 0 8
       ◇ Q 1 0 7 ◇ K 6 4 3
       ♣ K 9 8 ♣ 1 0 6 3 2

South	West	North	East
1NT	Dble	Pass	Pass
Pass			

Over 1NT, a double is for penalties, simply showing a stronger hand than the opener's. Knowing that his side has a clear edge in high cards and, having no very long suit to bid anyway, East is quite content to defend against 1NT doubled.

CONCLUSION

If you have worked your way through all the problems in this book, you are no doubt a good deal more tired than when you started. You can also be sure that you are now a much better bidder, with more understanding of, not only the rules, but also the reasons behind those rules.

You didn't get all of the problems right the first time through? That is hardly surprising. Concentrate on those areas in which you did badly until you can see where you were going wrong. You will come out all the better for the experience. Good luck.